GW01605173

MORLEY MATTERS

MORLEY MATTERS

ROBERT MORLEY

with a preface by *Peter Bull*

Robson Books

FIRST PUBLISHED IN GREAT BRITAIN IN 1980 BY ROBSON BOOKS LTD., 28 POLAND STREET, LONDON W1V 3DB.

ACKNOWLEDGEMENTS

Thanks are due to the editors and proprietors of the following publications in which some of these pieces originally appeared: *Punch, High Life,* the *Evening News* ('With Veils', 'The Happy Punter', 'Dukeophilia'), *Liverpool Daily Post* ('The Christmas Air Raid), *Playboy* ('Dressing to Kill'), *Tatler* ('Country Life').

Editor: Sheridan Morley

Morley, Robert
Morley matters.
I. Title
828 '.9' 1208 PN6175

ISBN 0-86051-115-4

Printed in Great Britain by R. J. Acford Ltd. Chichester

Phototypesetting by Georgia Origination, Liverpool

Contents

Preface by PETER BULL 7

Portraits and Portents

I'll Try Anything Once 13
With Veils 16
Her Husband and I 20
Pope Ruth 24

Brave New Worlds

It's All Goa 31
Western Approaches 35
Brave New Worlds 38
Los Angeles Nostalgia 43
The Doctor's Hat 46
Meeting the President 50
Life in Venice 56

Penmanship

All My Own Words 61
Dressing to Kill 64
Easy Reader 70

Treading the Boards

My Public 77
My Critics 80
My Agents 83
My Directors 87
My Scripts 92
Summing Up 96

Australasia Revisited

Kiwi Polish 101
Dateline Melbourne 104
Down Under and Out 109
The Starfish Encounter 114

Movable Feasts

The Worldwide Gourmet 121
Just My Cup of Tea 125
Don't Drink the Water 128

The Silver Screen

The Human Factor 135
Western Reproaches 138
If the Face Fits 141

The Happy Punter

Keeping an Eye on the Pressure 147
Death of a Snailsman 152
The Christmas Air Raid 155
The Contemporary Arthurian 158
Country Life 161
The Happy Punter 165
Life at the Big Top 168
Dukeophilia 172

Preface

As a *soi-disant* writer whose letter 'I' keeps on falling off the typewriter from over-use, it is a delighful chore to yack about someone else for a change, viz: my distinguished old friend, Robert Morley, Doc. Litt. (Reading University), a creative artist who appears never to run a similar risk.

In fact I was in New York recently and called up British Airways to check a flight and a familiar thick rich voice said, 'This is Robert Morley' and proceeded to pass on the info. through the blower without using the word 'I' once.

I first met him *circa* fifty years ago, when I was appearing in a play called *England Expects*, which was about Lord Nelson. In the programme it read 'A Sailor' Peter Bull and A Sailor had his great moment when he rushed on and announced to the dying Admiral that the *Leviathan* had been sunk. On a certain night I came on and said, 'Milord, the *Lusitania* has been sunk.' Stale news to the Coventry audience, and my lady agent who was among them. She came backstage after the performance, not unnaturally displeased by her client's contribution to the entertainment.

Her companion, on the other hand, gave me a charming smile and extended his hand saying, 'May I congratulate you on the worst performance I've ever seen on any stage? My name is Robert Morley.'

Of course we became great friends. And after one game of squash which I won and a few games of poker in which he won about £35,000 (in theory) we stopped all that sort of thing and settled down to the more serious fruits of our relationship – like starting the first American-type summer theatre in a Womens' Institute situated in a remote Cornish village. No salaries were dished out, but lodging and a good deal of board was. I sort of looked after the company and the takings, and Robert played practically all the leading parts in our first season. He proved a tower of strength and a formidable surfer.

One night a lady in the audience fell through her 2/4d upright deck-chair. She didn't hurt herself fortunately, or indeed sue us, but we decided to cut down on a similar risk. We instituted a curious ritual and nightly Robert, myself and another lovely large artiste, the late Judith Furse, used to test out every seat. Our ploy was to sit down and pretend to be helpless with (a) laughter and (b) terror, and bounce about like anything. If the canvas survived this ordeal, we felt considerably reassured.

Looking back, Robert seems to have cushioned and supported me in a variety of ways throughout the years. He wrote a delightful play about a repertory company for our summer theatre. It was called *Goodness, How Sad!* and we took it subsequently to London, where it got excellent reviews but failed to draw the town. After a month drastic steps had to be taken and the cast took huge cuts. The lessors of the Vaudeville Theatre let us have their building for £60 a week, which was just as well as we never took more than £500. Mr Morley not only forewent his royalties for the whole run of seven months but gave us enough money for the entire company to have a huge tuck-in at Rules restaurant on the first Monday night after we'd closed.

During the war I was on leave and one Saturday night was pretty keen to see *The Man Who Came To Dinner*, in which Robert had scored a triumph. The stage box was the only available accomodation left, from which the view was far from perfect. Mr Morley told an astonished cast that he wanted all the moves altered for that one performance so that my friends and I wouldn't miss any of the action. This pronunciamento caused confusion and a good deal of giggling on the stage, but vast contentment to Ordinary Seaman Bull and Party.

Memories come floating down the years of the bizarre occasions we have shared. I think very few prospective bridegrooms have spent the night before their wedding with a few friends at an A.B.C. in Islington consuming anything up to ten fishcakes with chips, before proceeding to Collins' Music Hall on the Green.

For one of his birthdays he hired several light aircraft to take a group of us over to Le Touquet for the day. The fact that there was a widespread strike throughout France that day didn't deter him in the least. Mysteriously the airport, a first class restaurant and the Casino opened their doors to Monsieur Morley, who gave us all the wherewithal to have a flutterette or *bijou flutter aux tables*.

He tends to turn up in my life on the most unexpected occasions. After the first night of John Osborne's *Luther* at the Sarah Bernhardt Theatre in Paris, he barged into my dressing-room, possibly drawn by the fact that I had been billed as 'Peter Dull' on the posters. He didn't care for the piece much but insisted on inviting me out to a chic restaurant. I demurred, as there was a heat wave on and I was dressed (to put it mildly) a trifle casually. Mr Morley cut a large bit out of my dressing-gown cord and constructed a peculiar bow tie out of it.

I have a tiny house on what was once a fairly remote Greek island. One Sunday afternoon I was awakened from my siesta by a voice yelling 'BULL' from about three-quarters of a mile away. It was Robert, who had hired a special caïque to bring him and his party over from Corfu, some four hours' steaming. He climbed my steep hill and, though the sparse amenities and reckless openings of every tin in the building weren't quite his glass of ouzo, he scored ten out of ten in my opinion for effort and show of friendship and loyalty.

He is a Gemini, of course, and persons born under that sign have boundless energy, which accounts for his prodigious output in acting, writing and generally living life to the full. He's made me laugh through all these media more than anyone I've ever known, and for this I am truly grateful. But I do think we should all give thanks to him for always being larger than life itself in this erratic era, and constantly surprising us by his rather dotty but always stimulating views on anything which takes his fancy. The violence of his political opinions and his devastating advice to the whole of the world on How-To-Do-It keeps us all on our toes. Long may he remain his unique self.

Ladies and Gentlemen, affectionately and with great confidence, let me present a little more of Morley.

PB

PORTRAITS AND PORTENTS

I'll Try Anything Once

Somewhere in the archives of the British Museum there should be one of my father's poems. He may have written others but if so I never read them. I know this one arrived at the museum because I posted it myself. My father gave me the envelope which contained his masterpiece printed at his own expense on cardboard and there was a loop of silk attached to affix it in a prominent position. Mind you, in the case of the museum I don't think Father ever believed it would be hung up. By law, he explained to me, everthing published has to go to the museum.

'But is it really published?' I asked him.

'Of couse, boy, printed and published by me and incidentally advertised by me in the agony columns of *The Times* this very morning.'

He drew my attention to the insertion for which presumably he had also forked out: 'Is there a life hereafter? Send a shilling postal order to Major Morley, The Firs, Rolvenden, Kent.'

Intriguing, one must admit, particularly as the poem itself seemed to be the account of a wedding and subsequent funeral of a young lady who habitually wore a violet corsage. Father was fond of violets.

My father never published again. 'There is simply no money in literature,' he was wont to remark, 'I tried it myself once. People just aren't interested.' I inherited from my father a love of gambling, making the sweeping statement and never being afraid of having a go—although the last precept I had little opportunity of putting into effect until my schooldays were behind me. In the schools I went to there was little opportunity of having a go unless you wished to be soundly thrashed almost immediately afterwards.

My father liked to boast he had tried everything once and some things, like bankruptcy, a number of times. He opened tea shops and night clubs, bred polo ponies and racing pigeons, started militant guerrilla bands in South Africa, held a commission in the Dragoon Guards and ever after retained his silver-plated helmet converted into a biscuit tin, another of his inventions which, alas, never caught on—and seemed to be perpetually clutching a hand of cards or a telephone connected to a bookmaker. It was his perpetual survival in fair health, and even better spirits, that heartened my own youth for the struggle to come.

Life for me really began, however, about thirty when most of the family were beginning to fear I had left it a bit late.

I had been an actor for nearly ten years and (as these were the days long before inflation) found it impossible, when I was not resting, as we called it, to get my weekly salary into double figures.

One morning I answered an advertisement not in *The Stage* but in the *Daily Telegraph* which invited applicants to call personally at an address in Bond Street which provided employment in an immensely attractive and lucrative field to willing lads with no previous experience of any kind. The first thing I saw when I entered the offices was a vacuum cleaner. 'Don't shy away from it,' the man sitting behind the desk advised. 'We pay while you train, give it a go.' I did just that, trudging the lanes and the avenues of Beaconsfield, ringing doorbells and trying to get my foot over the threshold. What you need in this game, I was told, is a good hat to take off and stout boots to act as a wedge.

The main trouble was that everyone already had a vacuum cleaner. My task was to get the customer to discard the one she had and go for novelty in the shape of what I learnt to describe as an entirely revolutionary domestic hygienic system. The revolution was in the plastic bubble in which the user could, if he wished, examine the dust atoms swirling around; they never actually went into the bag provided but gave at times a tolerable imitation of a paperweight being agitated to produce a snow storm. For the first few weeks I couldn't bring myself to believe anyone would be fool enough to fall for my foreplay and seldom got into the house, then one never-to-be-forgotten morning I sold two straight off and became a salesman, something I have remained ever since. Confidence is all—I went from strength to strength, was put in charge of a team, given a motor car and competed in inter-sales contests at monthly meetings. I even attended ceremonial prizegivings where hymns of praise were sung, admonishing the faithful. *Onward vacuum salesman, eager for the fray. Peal the bells and enter. Make the housewife pay*. Good stuff and in those days we had them more or less at our mercy and didn't have to state our business before the buzzer released the catch.

The money was good too, far better than that paid on yet another tour of *Charley's Aunt* which I found myself returning to with relief in due course. I had after all learnt my lesson in life, that there is what others less deeply in love than I with the common man might describe as the sucker element. The imponderable and unexpected rise of the fish to take the fly; how else to account for the fact that every now and again someone will answer their own front door and half an hour later have succumbed to the temptation offered by the sight of a new soap powder or a pair of panty hose. Big spenders may even sign up for *Encyclopaedia Britannica* and garden rollers. The truth once grasped, it seemed to me perfectly possible that a play I had written would be purchased straight or very nearly straight away by the leading comedy actress of her day. I more or less expected the phone to ring on the Monday morning summoning me to lunch and to discuss production after I had posted the script to her the previous Friday. So it proved. I was no longer surprised when given a star role, only astounded that it had previously been offered elsewhere.

To ensure such a state of affairs continuing I even became, with the help of trusted allies, an actor-manager. After three years my partners and I still had the prettiest offices in town, without a desk but with enormous sofas and an even larger dining table and the walls were hung with more than a dozen playbills as a reminder of our efforts and of the least complaining backers in the business. Like most managers we guessed it wrong three times out of four but those were heady days when in conference we would decide that Lord Olivier was too old for a part he would never have accepted anyway, and that I would be wise to play it myself.

It was the example of my own father which prompted me to say snap when the first offer was made, but it is to the housewives of Beaconsfield, who slammed the doors in my face and then one morning opened them unexpectedly, to whom I owe the deepest gratitude. They taught me, or just possibly I taught myself, that when pennies drop from heaven they fall into the lap of the faithful, the hopeful, the persevering. If you had told me all those years ago that behind the front doors of sensible villas lurk sensible matrons who can be persuaded every now and again in one single act of folly to get rid of a perfectly good cleaner and make a down payment on a new domestic hygienic system, so complicated that in my case at least I couldn't even demonstrate it efficiently, I wouldn't have believed you.

With Veils

Recently, my elder son Sheridan published his account of the life of his distinguished grandmother, Gladys Cooper, a woman I profoundly admired, loved and in whose company I rejoiced for thirty-three years without either ever knowing her really well or completely understanding her.

When Sheridan grew his first beard Gladys remonstrated that it made him look like a Russian Jew. 'You don't care for them?' I enquired coldly, for we allow no hint of criticism where our children are concerned.

'I have known a great many Russian Jews, Diaghilev for instance, and got on extremely well with them all. On the other hand Sheridan is neither Jewish nor Russian and I cannot for the life of me understand why he wants people to think he is,' she replied.

It was useless to point out that there comes a point in some men's lives when they throw in the towel along with the safety razor. Gladys was convinced that one of her grandsons was trying to be what he wasn't. She couldn't bear that sort of thing.

Yet, although she was often critical of what she believed to be nonsense in others, her own life was filled to the brim with it. Nonsense and high spirits had pulled her through. Kipling's great poem *If* could have been written for her. She filled the unforgiving minute, treated triumph and disaster like impostors, talked to crowds and kept her virtue, walked with kings and never lost the common touch. She was more like a man than Rex Harrison himself. Her story is the legend of a girl who started as a picture postcard and finished a Dame of the British Empire and in between danced with Valentino, had Greta Garbo to tea and to do the washing-up and made, as far as she was concerned, the supreme sacrifice in forgoing the chance of being the first woman to loop the loop because, as she always told us, she didn't wish to break up the pilot's marriage.

There have been two previous books published about her life: one, her autobiography published in 1931, which was largely ghosted by her half-sister and is in the form of miscellaneous anecdotes somewhat haphazardly slung together. I feel Gladys only looked over her half-sister's shoulder from time to time to see how the work was progressing and to volunteer additional material. Thus we learn that 'Mary Kinder was married first to Delaval Astley who was killed flying in Belfast before the war. Through him she inherited Chequers which was subsequently bought from her by Lord Lee and presented by him to the nation as a country house for Prime Ministers. Afterwards, she married a young man named Falcke who once tried to shoot himself while riding in a hansom cab with Iris Hoey.' One can see her hurrying off as she spoke the last line to attend to more urgent business, leaving her readers in some doubt, not of her disapproval of anyone being so foolish but whether Mr Falcke's actual misdemeanour lay in not finishing the job properly or in riding in a hansom with Miss Hoey.

My friend Mr Stokes's otherwise excellent biography, published twenty years later, had for me the somewhat misleading title *Without Veils*. In my experience she usually pulled down the blinds, let alone the veils, in order to retain a personal anonymity. She was the most private public figure I ever met and, if I never got to know her completely, I comforted myself with the belief that very few others did either. Perhaps her secret was that, while she was justifiably proud of her achievements in the world of the theatre and later the cinema, in a different and private world she was at odds with herself. She married three men each so utterly disparate from the others as to give the lie to the popular belief that those who change horse in midstream prefer to continue the journey by remounting a similar steed. She remembered two of her husbands with tolerant affection; the third she apparently failed to recognize when a few years after their separation they met at a christening of a mutual granddaughter. But I believe her heart belonged to the man she didn't marry but with whom she acted on many occasions, Gerald Du Maurier.

If I am right, we need not look far for the reason. The word charisma was surely invented to describe his quality. He had the irresistible melancholy of a high dignitary of the Church of Rome, combined with the studied calm and worldliness of a Greek banker at the baccarat table and, like Gladys herself, he wore elegance draped casually across his shoulders. Ever after their meeting the rest of us simply never measured up. Like most men whenever I try not putting my arms into the sleeves the garment falls to the ground.

Although Robert Hardy, Gladys's other son-in-law has marginally more elegance than I, we never quite satisfied her standards, though she made valiant efforts to disguise the truth, at any rate when we were present. Only once did her guard slip when the three of us were dining together and Gladys remarking on an acquaintance of hers who was experiencing family dissension repeated an observation she had made that afternoon. 'I said to her, my dear Mildred, if there is one thing you have to learn at your age it is to live with your sons-in-law. It is not the slightest use going out into the garden and pretending you are not at home, particularly now the winter is coming on.'

When towards the end of her long and valiant life she decided to come home and live near her family in Henley, I felt I might get to know her better. This was a time perhaps for the strands to come together, the jigsaw to be completed though I knew there would always be pieces of the puzzle which had gone missing but I hoped, perhaps, that she might sometimes take time off from the obsessional interest in chutney and marmalade forever bubbling on the stove to fill in the picture if not for others, then for herself. It is true that once she stood beside me at Ascot when the great Arkle was being unsaddled in the winners' enclosure in the presence of the umpteenth Duchess of Westminster.

'Could have been mine!' she remarked suddenly.

'Did the late Duke propose then?' I asked.

'All the time, of course if I'd known about Arkle, I might have said yes.'

Yet her attitude to possessions was ambivalent. She was constantly adding outhouses to the garden in which to store chests newly arrived from America crammed with old photographs and theatre programmes, collapsed armchairs and swimming pool filtration equipment salvaged from the home she had once built for herself in Santa Monica. Her Thunderbird also came from the USA. She spent a fortune on freight charges. More important perhaps to the inhabitants of Henley it had a left-hand drive and, whenever Gladys alighted and forgot to close the door, all traffic in the High Street was halted. Then, sadly, it was all over. Miss Cooper reluctantly cancelled the remaining dates of a tour of *The Chalk Garden* and went into hospital. The doctors withheld their diagnosis and prescribed heroin and Gladys who had never allowed herself the indulgence of a single aspirin looked forward to her daily shot. 'Don't know what it is, dear,' she told me, 'but it seems to be doing me no end of good.' On the last evening she took what was for her an exceptionally long look into the mirror and on the way back to bed said to her nurse, 'If this is what pneumonia does for people, I don't really think I shall bother to have it again.' She died of cancer on 17 November 1971.

In her memory we rebuilt a gazebo on the banks of the Thames she loved and added an inscription. A few weeks later the plaque to her memory was stolen. I don't think she would have given a hoot. 'They can still sit there can't they?' she would have asked. But then again with darling Gladys one can never be quite sure.

Her Husband and I

How well did I know the Duke of Windsor? It's a question which I have up to now been inclined to duck, to use a term of which HRH himself was fond. He in his own pond was always ducking and, of course, when he finally ducked the crown I had been half-expecting him to do so. Indeed, I remember wasting a few shillings in a private recording booth to make my own version of his abdication speech long before the event took place and, whenever a ring on the doorbell sounded, I would play it while ushering my guests up to the bed-sitting-room I occupied in those days.

'Great things are happening,' I would urge, 'don't talk, just listen.'

I always thought my own farewell sounded a good deal more moving than his but, of course, he was never to hear it.

I was not to meet the Duke of Windsor (as he was by then known) until some years later, and nowadays when so much is still being written and watched on television and on stage about him, I feel I should no longer keep to myself the story of how we finally became acquainted and to throw what light I can on this eccentric and enigmatic character.

Very well then, the scene is the Lido, that narrow stretch of sand bordering the Adriatic, one of the numerous islands which share with Venice herself (I imagine the Queen of Cities must be feminine) the lagoon. While some of these islands are given over to lace-making and glass-blowing and one to nothing very much but eating luncheon, the Lido itself (because of its fine sandy beach which compares favourably with our own Weston-Super-Mare) provides in the short summer season a refuge for the successful rich. The two states are by no means synonymous. It is quite possible to be successful and poor or unsuccessful and extremely wealthy. But in the years of which I write, and during one of which I encountered the Duke and Duchess, most of us stretched out in front of our *cabanas* had little to worry about except sunburn.

It may help my readers to understand what exactly occurred at the historic tea party, the circumstances of which I am about to relate, if I were to fill them in with the conditions which in those days prevailed on the sands. The Lido was not the sort of place where anyone could simply stroll on to the beach, drop their trousers and wade into the water. The foreshore was reserved almost exclusively for the patrons of the two principal hotels, Des Bains and the Excelsior. Early on the day of your arrival you paid a large sum to the *concierge des plages* or indicated you were willing for it to be added to your bill; you were then allotted a *cabana* which contained two upright chairs and two day beds, a limited supply of towels and a sunshade. Occupants of the *cabana* were limited to six in number and any attempt to spill over into an adjacent beach lot was sternly resisted, not only by the occupants but, if they were absent, by guards who constantly patrolled the dividing catwalks which led to the communal toilets, showers and the restaurant whither everyone resorted between 2.00 and 3.30.

Hidden discreetly from our view was the field hospital and the children's playground. The hospital dealt with burns, stings and heart attacks. The children's playground was little patronized. During the afternoon all games were banned from the sea shore and, although during the morning it was permissible to erect fortifications and scoop out paddling pools, the sand was conscientiously levelled at intervals, not by the waves, as is normally the case on such locations, but by a positive army of attendants who at the same time removed seaweed, transported shells and the occasional ice-cream paper.

Italian children have always struck me as being extremely old for their age and, although one occasionally came across a small group of them chattering in the shade behind the huts, their behaviour was quite different from the kind of rowdy exhibitionism normally encountered on an English beach. An Italian parent, for instance, never throws a ball at his or her offspring or exhorts him to run races or comb hair. In point of fact, all Italians of whatever sex or age, I find, comb it to excess. My own children (who have never cared for games) were perfectly happy in the water, hiring beach floats, purchasing ice-cream, (or anything in fact which cost money) spotting Henry Fonda in the distance and waiting for the sun to set and life to begin. Towards dusk, they would disappear up the road opposite the Excelsior where the action was or was likely to start at any moment. They were not in the least upset therefore when one afternoon we explained to them that they could get away a bit early and see if there were any returns for the latest Peter Sellers epic while we were bidden to tea with Wallis and David.

The Windsors were not themselves giving the party but their hosts rented the next cabin. There can be no harm, surely, after all these years in revealing their name—Peter, now I am happy to say, Lord Thorneycroft and his Italian wife who was also, of course, his English wife. This is the place, surely, to interpolate a story about HRH and my father-in-law who owned a club in London of which the Prince was patron. As sometimes happens, they had fallen out when HRH had resisted some suggestion of my father-in-law's with the phrase, 'Buck (his name was Buckmaster) don't try and hang your hat on me.' My father-in-law was not wearing a hat, (naturally as the exchange took place in his own lavatory) and was at a loss to understand what was meant at the time. Later, when it was explained to him, he was very angry indeed, and for some years the two only acknowledged each other's presence with a brief nod. One evening at the Embassy (what a pleasure it is to recall the old names, but for new readers this is not to be confused with an embassy, the Embassy was a night club in Bond Street, indeed I believe it is to this day), he was shown to a table next to the Prince. His Royal Highness was all smiles, 'Buck, my dear fellow,' he greeted him, 'I want you to meet Mrs Simpson.'

'And I, sir,' replied Buck, indicating his own companion, 'would like you to meet *Miss* Simpson.' The last time they met on the golf course at Sunningdale, the Prince drove straight through without even nodding. You can't, as my father-in-law was fond of observing, expect to win them all.

When we asked the Thorneycrofts at what hour we were to present ourselves, my wife and I were told to do so soon after the other guests arrived. No exact hour had been fixed as they were coming by bus. I must say that was quite a surprise. Somehow I couldn't see them in a bus and, of course, I didn't. The bus stops on the upper road and the pair found their own way along the cat-walk and joined our hosts. We counted, or rather I did, seven hundred and fifty slowly (I had decided previously on the number), and then walked across and were introduced. I recall that the Prince was not wearing a coat. I recall that, after a time, I returned to our *cabana* for our chairs and that Mrs Simpson herself handed me a cup of tea. Of the rest of the encounter my mind is completely blank.

I have in my time had occasion to speak with several other members of the Royal Family and can recall exactly what was said. Why then cannot I remember what occurred on the early autumn afternoon while the shadows of two such august personages continued to lengthen on the sands of time? I cannot explain it except to think there was some sort of magic about the couple which confused and at the same time obliterated memory, hence the countless books and utterly divergent plays and films which continue to pour from our presses and screens. All I know is they went home as they came and we wondered if they found seats. The buses are crowded at that time of day.

Pope Ruth

The surprise appointment of Mrs Ruth Grazely of Cirencester as the new Pope was, of course, foreshadowed by the interview Father Greeley of Chicago gave in a press conference last month when he urged that the next Pope should not only be a woman but one who laughs a good deal. 'The more she laughs, the more effective she will be,' he added.

Nor could the news have astonished Mr Coudenove Kalergi who writing to *The Times* the other day pointed out that in the last one hundred and thirty years a lean pope whose name did not contain the letter R was always followed by a stout one with an R to his name.

When I drew Mrs Grazely's attention to this pronouncement her only comment was she didn't altogether believe in that nonsense but in any case it was lucky she hadn't joined Weight Watchers when urged to do so by her family. Pope Ruth, as she intends to be known, has five children and a husband.

'All the more surprising really,' she remarked, 'seeing that I am not or at least haven't been in the past a Catholic. I've been to their services, of course, every now and again, usually abroad when my husband and I were sightseeing—there's nearly always a service going on at the far end.

'Of course I'll have to get to know the far end a bit better from now on,' she laughed merrily. 'Fortunately the children are growing up and I am sure there'll be no shortage of baby sitters in the Vatican. The trouble with the Vatican as I see it, and I am speaking only from the photographs they have shown me, is that there is a good deal too much stuff lying around, some of it apparently very valuable. It might be better to put some of it in store until my youngest starts school – she is a terrible little fidget and I don't fancy having to replace some of those crucifixes and then, of course, there are the vestments – we don't want her dressing up in those.'

Asked how she saw her new job all Mrs Grazely would admit is that it would be a nice change from hand laundering of which she was heartily sick. 'And so is Bert,' she admitted. Her husband drives the van and apparently had sometimes to rise at five in the morning. I pointed out to her that the late Pontiff often rose at that hour and she seemed surprised. What on earth, she wondered, had he found to do so early. Pray, I told her.

'Ah,' observed Mrs Grazely, 'well I certainly shan't be doing that. In point of fact I rather relish a good lie-in. So does Bert. If I had a criticism of my predecessor, it would be that he prayed too much. I take the view that the Almighty has heard it all by now and what he'd like us to do is to get on with ourselves. I am hoping my reign, if that doesn't sound too la-di-da, will be more like the Queen Mum's. Very few people ever saw her praying except when it was necessary in the Abbey or somewhere. No, she gets about the Queen Mum does and that's what I intend to do. You know, one of the nicest things about her is when she goes round inspecting cottage gardens and chatting up the OAPs. That's the sort of thing I should like to do, visiting the patients in hospitals and then just enjoying myself. I want everyone to enjoy themselves so I reckon I had better set an example.'

I enquired whether we might expect Her Holiness on the race track.

'Who knows? That sort of thing would bring the Church out into the open and if only I could get the right horses the faithful might make a bob or two. There would be no harm in that and, of course, if they wished they could give a bit back to the Church.'

Mrs Grazely also revealed for the first time how her selection came about. 'It all started as a joke,' she laughed. 'My husband happened to see this bit in the paper. *Wanted a hopeful, holy man who can smile. Interesting work guaranteed. Income, residence comes with position. Protection from proven security organization.* "That's you, Ruth," he told me. Of course it was Father Greeley just putting out a feeler. In an advertisement he wouldn't have been allowed to put Holy Man it would have to have been Holy Person. Anyway, I wrote in and applied and it seems this time the cardinals didn't want to be caught napping. They're all getting on and rather than spend hours lighting that chimney they put all the applicants into a computer. I mean, of course, the forms not the actual people. Ho Ho. Greeley put mine in as a bit of a joke but I expect he's laughing on the other side of his face now. Still as long as he is laughing, that's the main thing, isn't it?' And once more Her Holiness let forth a bellow of mirth.

How about birth control then, I asked, do you see any difficulty there?

'It's always a difficulty,' she told me, 'otherwise we should probably have stopped ourselves at three. Still I don't intend to be dogmatic. Carry on, I shall tell them, and use your nonce.'

On ecumenicity the Holy Mother was more cautious. 'What we all have to avoid in times like these,' she told me, 'is redundancies and what we must conserve is freedom of choice. I go along with Margaret Thatcher on that one. Now there's a girl who would have made a smashing Pope but I suppose Denis didn't put her up to it like my old man did. Maybe he didn't want her gallivanting about to foreign parts.'

Would Her Holiness be doing a lot of travelling?

'Rather!' she told me. 'That's what makes the job so exciting. I may not have been to church much but I wouldn't mind going round the world.

'My job is to talk to people, ask them why they don't go to church and see if we can't give them what they want. It's called consumer research. Bert used to be very keen on that when he called with the laundry baskets. He used to ask them outright how they liked their pyjamas folded or whether there was too much starch in their dickeys, then he would pass the message on and we had another satisfied customer. That's what I want as Pope, satisfied customers. A lot of them believe, you know, that they'll get their reward in Heaven. Don't bank on it! Could be, could be not, but there's no reason why we shouldn't have a bit of fun while we're waiting to find out.'

I asked Pope Ruth whether she was in favour of allowing the clergy to marry.

'Why not indeed?' she replied. 'And have children. They always used to in the old days, you know.'

'How long ago was that?' I asked but Pope Ruth contorted her features without speaking.

'That's the one thing I have never been able to do,' she told me. 'I have never been able to wink, my efforts at winking are pathetic. But to go back to your question, I shall positively encourage matrimony. There are far too many drop-outs for my liking where marriage is concerned nowadays. I am planning a little bull,' she gave a nervous chuckle, 'a little bull setting out my plans to get the show on the road again. At the moment we are definitely holed up in our winter quarters and we must get moving. Not every priest wants to marry or cardinal either—they have too good a life being waited on by the sisters of charity.'

Her Holiness is keenly looking forward to her enthronement early next month. 'It's going to be quite a thrash,' she told us, 'guests coming from all over the world. I won't tell you what I am going to wear but it will be different. As for the cardinals, I would like to get rid of all those extraordinary costumes and hats—in my opinion they put more people off than they turn on.

'I shall have the ceremony indoors. It's no good building a church like St. Peter's and then having everything take place outside – to my mind it shows a lack of confidence. My predecessor, you know, had his burial service in the square. He had told them to keep it simple so they just laid the coffin down on the ground, no flowers, no candles, nothing. That's what it looked like on television. I can imagine what Sir Lew Grade must have thought of it.

'It's very close in here, don't you think?' she observed and rose to open a window.

No doubt this indomitable lady will be opening a good many before she has finished. I took my leave feeling curiously reassured. There is always a great deal to be said for appointing an Englishman or, in this case, an Englishwoman to preside over an institution of which he or she has little, if any, knowledge. It has worked with the Post Office, it's worked with the Milk Board and the *Daily Express* and I feel pretty certain it's going to work for Catholics.

BRAVE NEW WORLDS

It's All Goa

Normally I'm as eager as the next man to find whither I am bound. In my time I have spent a fortune on guide books, potted histories, small and large scale maps and personal accounts by other intrepid explorers who live to tell the tale after a summer among the Basque people. The decision to spend a week on Goa was reached precipitously when a friend rang up and invited me to complete a party of four planning to spend a week mudlarking in the Arabian Sea. 'I am your man,' I told her, looked up my vaccination certificate (for we are now the last smallpox risk in the world) and boarded a jumbo that very evening for Bombay.

'From Bombay to Goa,' I enquired, over the complimentary champagne, 'how do you envisage the journey?'

'By plane,' she told me.

'But surely,' I argued, 'your son and his girlfriend travelling in the economy section will be anxious to see as much of India as possible. We must go by road.'

Sitting in the Taj Mahal Hotel that evening I made the necessary arrangements or, to be accurate, my friends had already made them but the gentleman from the travel agency had expressed a desire to meet me personally. It was apparently one of his lifelong ambitions to meet an actor whom he had admired for so long on the silver screen. I make no apology for simply repeating his words. Those of us who know our India will realize that all that has been written about the singular faithfulness of character ascribed in so many novels to the bearer boy, Sepoy, Pathan, servant and village headman still holds today. I don't say the travel wallah was actually waiting for his master's return on the tarmac but here he was with a glass of whisky in his hand, closely questioning me on the various roles I had played, with particular emphasis on a rather early work of mine, *The Final Test*, which dealt with the game so dear to the Indian heart.

He also was the director of an amateur group of players who frequently delighted Bombay with revivals of English drawing-room comedies, the presentation (or at least the casting) of which presented certain difficulties in that they did not lend themselves to the present trend for multi-racialism on the boards.

He was anxious for us to begin our travel as early as possible in the excellent motor he had secured, together with a driver fluent in the English tongue, and suggested we should assemble in the entrance hall at six, having not partaken of too much breakfast as a particularly fine one would be awaiting us at Poona.

'Now that is a place I have always wanted to see,' I told him as we bade him goodnight and fortified ourselves in the Golden Dragon with an elaborate Chinese Szechwan dinner, preparatory for our early morning fast. From the window of my bedroom I later gazed down on one of those unfinished office blocks whose state of uncertainty was emphasized by the squatters who had invaded the building. On the roof a family was putting the final touches to a hastily erected shack of rush matting by affixing an inverted U-bend lavatory pan to serve as a chimney.

Around the hotel, in a frieze of horror, beggars paraded armless children and mindless babies were laid out on the pavement and packaged in cellophane. The tourists cushion themselves from shock by telling each other that begging is a profession and a profitable one at that. On the whole, Bombay is a good place to be leaving at six in the morning or indeed at any other time.

The car seemed smaller than the occasion demanded but there is always a great advantage in being large for one's age; it means you can say, 'I'd better sit in front otherwise I might crowd you,' and no one argues. The idea of Poona, however, did not appeal to the driver whom, if I understood correctly—and for the next sixteen hours I understood very little of what he said or indeed was trying to do—seemed to think lay in a different direction from Goa. On the other hand he gave very little indication that he knew in what direction Goa lay and none whatever that he could change gears without first stopping the car and starting from scratch or, perhaps more properly, from grind. At the rate of forty kilometres an hour we made slow progress but arrived at about twelve in the little town of Mahad, where our driver stopped the car in the main street, effectively blocking traffic in four directions, and departed in search of a repair kit for his gearbox.

The initial curiosity of the inhabitants gave way to irritation at the thoughtlessness of our behaviour in bringing life to a standstill; we thought it prudent to abandon the car and explore the market. Normally my companion is a keen shopper but she found little on the stalls to attract her. Suffering from a slight stomach upset, she went in search of a public convenience and was not to meet up with one for another ten hours, though I did persuade her later to seek out a private place by the side of the road while I stood by to repel Pathans and, of course, snakes. It was not for her, I am afraid, a happy situation, but as I pointed out we *were* seeing India and after a time the village grew comparatively silent as far as motor horns were concerned and we came upon our driver who, having mended the gearbox (at least to his satisfaction) was now parked in the square, exchanging wheel for wheel.

Another hour and we were on our way but relationships had subtly changed between us and him. He was now the master and realized he held the whip hand. For the rest of the interminable journey, whenever one of us was to question him too keenly as to our exact whereabouts and how much longer our journey might take, he invariably replied that we were now within a few miles of our destination. If we showed disbelief and remarked that a journey scheduled for nine hours had already taken twelve, he would stop the car abruptly, alight and inspect the tyres to remind us that we had no spare and only his goodwill to enable us to carry on.

Long after darkness fell, he continued to play on our nerves and although progress was slow along mountain passes, given a straight stretch of road or a village he accelerated, boldly contriving near-misses with laden ladies carrying vast bundles of water or food on their heads or buffalo attempting to cross his path. Eventually, and as it turned out only some fifteen kilometres from Fort Aguada Beach resort, whither we were bound, we found a taxicab stalled by the roadside. 'You are now under my protection,' I told the cabby kindly. 'Take your place beside our driver and direct him on the last stage of his journey. He is a stranger in these parts and has already made so many enemies on the road that no one but you can show the way. You will, of course, be handsomely rewarded.'

Half an hour later we were safe in the hotel lavatories and preparing to celebrate New Year around the swimming pool with the customary curry buffet and two bottles of champagne. I thought ordering the latter was a wise precaution as we had no reservations and would show an intention to push the boat out in the highly unlikely event of us being awarded accommodation. Finally, after the fireworks, we were all safely tucked up in one bedroom and the next morning allotted superior accommodation with patios and separate bedrooms.

The Aguada Fort has much to recommend it, particularly if you like sunbathing, curry and coconut milk and scrupulously clean surroundings. It is pleasantly over-staffed and serves excellent gin fizzes around the pool and there are miles and miles of sandy beach and a warm and unpolluted ocean.

There are at least three passable restaurants to be reached by taxi, of which possibly the best and most curious is St. Anthony's, about twelve miles along the beach and in a village regarded as the hippie centre of these parts.

The other two restaurants to which we repaired were the O Conquerio, where we were offered little to eat save stewed chicken, and the Gazelle at Panaji, which is Indian owned but serves very good European dishes including crayfish steak *au poivre* and lemon *soufflé*.

Well worth a visit, as indeed is Panaji itself. About five miles further along the river is the ancient Portuguese capital abandoned because of the prevalence of the mosquito now mercifully absent from the entire coast. Here in Bom Jesus Basilica lie the mutilated remains of Saint Francis Xavier. Mr Fodor notes drily that both big toes were bitten off by female fanatics and a arm severed at the request of a pope and sent to Rome. Still, it all looks very impressive and so does the St. Assisi Church and Convent opposite, now serving as a museum, and the Cathedral, in one of the chapels of which the vision of Christ is said to have appeared as late as 1919.

All in all a most enjoyable holiday. It should perhaps be recommended only to hardened travellers, who even proceeding by air from Bombay must expect a wait of an hour and a half before crossing the river by motor ferry. They must also not be put off the spectacle, glimpsed from the bus window, of young women ceaselessly toiling with iron bars to dislodge rust from the steel girders waiting to be erected when the new bridge is built.

'Conditions were almost as bad in Spain,' we tell each other, 'and look what we did for the place once the package tour industry got going.' But the Malabar Coast is not, alas, the Costa Brava.

Western Approaches

The musical *Annie* packed them in at the Shubert Theatre in Century City. The tale of an orphan child suddenly adopted by a multi-billionaire in the era when Roosevelt was President is a bedtime story of which no American ever tires. Roosevelt's famous dogma that America has nothing to fear save fear itself, and the insistence of Annie's benefactor that he personally never bothered to be nice to people on the way up as he has no intention of ever coming down, delights the entire house and would the whole nation if they could afford the twenty dollars it costs for a ticket to see the fun.

It is impeccable fun, beautifully staged, disciplined and unflagging. Like all American musicals it is the distillation of the talent that abounds in this country. Annie is already a star at eleven. Her fellow orphans are as cleverly trained, and as beautifully disciplined a bunch of moppets as ever came out of North Korea. Not that these are Korean children, but it just so happens that local reporters are currently back from Asia with rather disturbing shots of North Korean children who apparently perform prodigies of athletic skill and schoolroom studies from the age of nineteen months, when lessons start.

There is no connection between what is going on in the two countries, the problems facing Korea are not those facing America—not in North Korea at any rate—and the newsreels are careful to show the contrast between the prosperous South, with the traffic blocks and streets crowded with busy citizens out to make a quick buck, and the deserted capital up North with hardly a soul on the streets and no cars, just these strange new children, described by the commentator as the kings and queens of a new emerging nation, incomparably better dressed and housed than their parents, if indeed they have any, for one is given the impression that these too are orphans.

The American orphan is of course not nearly so appealing as the Korean variety. For one thing he is a good deal older and for another almost certainly armed and not averse, given the opportunity, to assault and battery, even murder, for the contents of a single wallet selected by chance on the sidewalks, which is one of the reasons why there are few pedestrians out after dark in Beverly Hills. The very occasional footstep such as my own occasions horrendous barking from behind the scrupulously maintained fences. Only the knowledge that they are in such perfect and necessary order gives me, at any rate, the courage to proceed and, even so, whenever possible I step on grass rather than pavement recalling a similar journey to school made more than sixty years ago when I would hasten, head bent, along the ditch to avoid a canine enemy alerted to my passing.

The main preoccupation of the citizen, however, is not highway robbery or even the current ominous cliff slides further along the coast, which has closed the State Pacific highway and made life complicated for the commuters stranded on the other side and now forced to travel by ferry boat. It is the fear that soon all must take to the water and row, or to their feet and walk, because the petrol simply isn't there any more or, what is worse, is there but comes and goes like a spring which is about to run dry for ever.

Motorists no longer drive where they choose but where they believe the last petrol pump still serves the customers. The name of the game is topping up, no matter how long it takes or how many lines of fellow motorists must be joined to ensure that your tank also receives its meagre ration. There are other more nefarious ways of ensuring your supply. Just as in the old days of Prohibition each man had his own supplier, so the black market has already mysteriously established itself. The baron's henchmen are out, armed with rubber hoses to siphon off the precious spirit. Youths who have not worked for some time or as yet perfected the technique of avoiding filling their own stomachs with petrol, hurry to casualty wards to be pumped dry in their turn.

The President brought little comfort. 'It's all going to get worse,' he told us cheerfully, and was photographed on an early morning jog with his Mexican host, a prosperous government employee in whose humble house, or as some pointed out not quite so humble as all that, he had stayed overnight. With the smell of panic replacing the customary whiff of oil, the elevation of the Blessed Margaret has struck for some at least a reassuring note. Where America leads, Britain is at last reluctantly prepared to follow. Who knows, the country slowed down by the Welfare State mentality of former leaders may now, if not exactly catch up, break into a gentle jog itself. But where to, is the question increasingly posed around these parts. Is it conceivable we are all headed in the wrong direction?

It is impossible not to admire what has been achieved, what is still being achieved here and, if happiness still eludes the pursuers, what fun has been had along the way. Nowhere has man had such a whale of a time and,if one day it all comes to an end as everything must, it was a brave effort. Perhaps the bravest effort man ever made to conquer his environment, to totally deny nature, to create not only a new landscape but, thanks to the internal combustion engine, a new climate. To invent smog itself, to insist that nothing was sacred, and that there was no plot of earth which could not be improved or built upon or at least bear the proud message of an airline or a mortuary.

'We tried three,' proclaims a young American whose bereavement is already lightened by the reassurance afforded by the morticians of Forest Lawn. 'This was the cheapest.' It is his and our triumphant conclusion. It sums it all up: when you've got to go, you've got to go.

Brave New Worlds

Tell me, Mr Morley, all those years ago when you were a struggling babe in your nurse's arms, did you ever believe that one day you would possibly have a soup named after you? The answer must be no – there is no reporter to pose the question, but I make bold to answer in advance. The details are not settled as yet; even the exact flavour of the soup is still to be decided, though I urged strongly for the one into which apricot jam is spooned—the jam perhaps in a separate tin skilfully attached and with enough residual to allow for a sandwich.

Throughout these vast Australian farmlands, I am known not as that serious dramatic artiste whose Lear is still awaited by eager critics but simply as Mr Heinz. Children lift their heads from their surf-boards, musos from their music score, darters from their cans of Fosters, to wave a greeting as I pass.

Even Warren Mitchell knows why I am here and is green with jealousy. He too used to advertise soup once upon a time, and now he is forced into actually giving them his Lear and his Willy Loman in *Death of a Salesman*. How ironic life can be. Otherwise Sydney wears that curious air of slap-happiness as is its wont. Even my accountant wears blue shorts, knee-length socks and sleeveless tunic with kerchief knotted at neck, reminding me of an uncle who was always the scoutmaster, or that solitary figure who some years ago represented rational dress in Threadneedle Street but is now alas, seen no more.

Rational dress is frowned on at Randwick for the races, formality is demanded. Hats and gloves for the ladies, long trousers for the gentlemen; there are only two things Australians take seriously, the other being Joan Sutherland. Each morning the newspapers carry her picture on the front page with an account of her latest contractual problems. Either she will sing Taglione at the Opera House in the autumn or she won't. Meanwhile, the question of whether she will fulfil her contract at the Metropolitan depends as always on whether she will be permitted to give her Merry Widow.

Miss Sutherland is always smiling, in the picture at least; beside her is her bearded husband and conductor looking very cross indeed. Further into the pages is Warren. A smaller picture of him but looking equally annoyed. There is a row about the way they sell or rather don't sell theatre tickets at his box offices. Thirty years ago I too enquired about the custom of not keeping them on the premises. Too valuable, they told me – I have puzzled over the answer ever since.

Pay a courtesy call on Warren who has managed to sell a few tickets after all. One of those modern theatres in the round where I always expect to be able to hear and never do. Warren in the guise of Alf Garnett while he rehearses forthcoming attractions. Not a crowd exactly but he has been over the course rather often. He looks like a pickled walnut, a genuine gypsy who has sold an astonishing number of clothes-pegs over the footlights and years.

Spend an uncomfortable day in a cornfield plagued by flies and meeting myself dressed as a scarecrow, and an idyllic one on the Hawkesbury River under the shade of a gigantic fig-tree fishing off the pier in the company of two small boys who will try and help me to my feet whenever I have to rise. We always end in a heap with them underneath but luckily their parents are not there to apprehend the danger that I may squash them both.

There are two hundred miles of waterways round here, mostly national park, some of the most beautiful country I have ever seen and houseboats one can hire for a song. What are the things one should look for especially? I ask the water man. Black snakes and trapdoor spiders, he tells me. Just as the taxi-drivers in New York used to dramatize the muggings, so the Australians pinpoint the hazards. Jelly-fish, sharks, spiders, unidentified Turks wrapped in carpets and discovered on rubbish heaps by children searching for string, fill the pages of the press and make a welcome change from our own domestic problems.

On my last morning I lunch with Warren and Tarquin Olivier, the great man's son who sells banknotes throughout the Far East and tells us he is always at home in Hong Kong for the first week of the month. I leave them working out a schedule for Warren who wonders if the Mandarin Hotel is ready for *Lear*.

Tarquin still boasts of being the only man who ever kicked Gladys

Cooper out of bed, or so she told him when he achieved the feat at the age of five. She had unwisely shared a bed with him, a restless sleeper and her godson, at Frinton one summer when accommodation was short.

Leaving Sydney in the afternoon, one is still in time for a corned-beef-hash breakfast the same morning in Los Angeles. Thus gaining a day as well as weight.

Fly out to Vegas with a laudable intention of seeing the shows and not so much of the green baize, an ambition achieved largely because the money runs out sooner with the double zero.

How much America still owes to Walt Disney! In the Hilton there are five different restaurants in each of which the staff manfully pretend to be a separate ethnic group. There is a whole Japanese complex with Disney-animated singing birds and water jets and everything from raw fish to Kobi steaks individually massaged while still on the hoof. There is a Bavarian Beer House with the waiters in lederhosen (it is difficult to keep staff here, the head waiter affirms, because of the costume) and there is an English Rib Room with the girls dressed as if at any moment they expected to be called on to the set of *Upstairs*, or rather *Downstairs*. There are singing Italian waiters and traditional gourmet dining with *matelots* opening shellfish.

The Hilton Showroom, however, is all American: Lou Rawls and Tina Turner—names new to me but not to the platter people, the cassette clan. Here, buttock to buttock, we are packed at long tables for the obligatory four drinks at the cost of nineteen dollars for which instant payment is demanded by a waitress shining a red torch on your nostrils which she grips in her mouth. The torch, of course, not your nose.

A recorded warning against taking photographs precedes a show in which, alas, there was little to see except an orchestra on stage which eventually struck a chord signalling the arrival of Miss Tina disguised in an Afro wig which after her first number she discarded in a powder flash. A pleasant, noisy child who had not yet decided whether to grow up as Shirley MacLaine or Mae West, backed by two young men and their girl friends making loud noises and rude gestures. A pleasant walk-up-and-down comedian obliged, while the orchestra discarded trumpets for violins, and Mr Rawls himself, who relies on nostalgia and continuous enquiries about whether we are having a good time. On the whole I thought the general feeling was that we weren't, despite an elaborate backcloth which was dropped halfway through the act depicting Chicago as it might have been when he was young and so cold he had to wear galoshes in bed.

There is a good deal more fun to be had at the Desert Inn with Anthony Newley and Juliet Prowse, and at Caesar's Palace Sammy Davis Junior still works a room better than anyone in the world except Sinatra. Almost the best and certainly the most economical way of catching the shows is staying tuned every morning to the *Mike Douglas Television Show* on which they all appear together with visiting firemen intent on drawing your attention to their recent films. Mr Douglas has the unique gift of making them extremely entertaining while in his company and cutting out a good deal of the schmalz. The spectacle of Burt Reynolds charging round the audience on a scavenger hunt trying to divest the ladies of their wigs, panty hose and false teeth and collecting a half-eaten sandwich all in the space of two minutes, was one I shall cherish for some time. He was, of course, one hundred per cent successful.

Most successful of all perhaps is the extravaganza at MGM entitled *Hallelujah Hollywood* which opened here all of five years ago and is still the most spectacular revue I have ever seen introduced, and I refer to the marvellous, glorified, magnificent beauties of the Grand Hotel, besides Leo the living lion, a more than competent performing elephant and a brief appearance by a caravan of llamas and camels. But the highlights of the show are The Elevators, an uncanny group of orang-utans who take complete charge of their trainer, a Mr Bersoni, and a juggler who expels ping-pong balls a hundred feet in the air and catches them again in his mouth. My theory that he had previously swallowed an air pump was discounted by the head waiter at Caesar's Palace Spanish Restaurant, the best in town, who also urged me to visit the Lido Show at the Stardust where Siegfried and Roy now make an elephant disappear into thin air along with the lions and tigers with which they have been working their act for eleven years.

Halfway through their announcement that this evening they were privileged to be performing in front of a great star of the entertainment world, and preparatory to rising to my feet to greet the customary spotlight and the implied assurance that my check would be taken care of, I became aware they weren't speaking of me at all but a fellow conjuror who shared the table and who subsequently took me behind the scenes to be introduced to this legendary pair and their tigers, a couple of whom, still learning the business, sit unleashed on the stage during the proceedings.

I did not, of course, discover how this intrepid German pair do the tricks but was introduced to some of the cast and discovered the reason why they remain Vegas-bound. It is partly the money—who else, they ask, could afford to pay us?—but mostly because they and their pets live in a *ménage de tigres* only eight minutes away from the hotel and where all of them share the rumpus room and swim daily in the pool. There is only one of the bathers I have to watch, Siegfried explains and that, of course, is Roy. On a recent holiday in Bali they left their pets behind and disaster struck as the tigers went on hunger strike; all packed to return forthwith, they suddenly bethought themselves of the telephone and with the aid of loud speakers around the pool were able at prodigious cost to reassure the animals twice a day and get them to eat up.

Vegas is still the place for my money in more senses than one even when, as happened this time, it started to snow; not least perhaps because I remember the town the way it was back in '38 when Boulder Dam was still a-building and a clip from the then current *Vegas Sun* records that 'the number of people now on relief is gradually lessening as various government programmes enable men to work on the beautification of our city parks, and a big drive by the Catholic Church is going on nationally to clean up movies coming from Hollywood. There is some reason for the concern of the motion picture industry's effect on morals. The country is indeed plagued by gangsters, although local crime has lessened despite the road to the dam continuing to attract a disagreeable element.' The paper, alas, noted that the schoolhouse had been burnt down yet again and the children had gone back to their studies in ten tents measuring twenty-four feet by forty feet each.

It is just like thirty years ago when all America went to school. Will we ever be without tents in Las Vegas?

Los Angeles Nostalgia

It is years and years ago since the Brown Derby and Mike Romanoff's and Schrafts little hot cakes. Yet when I was first in Los Angeles and staying at the Beverly Wiltshire (courtesy Metro-Goldwyn-Mayer) in order to test for the role of the dauphin in *Marie Antoinette* my agent would call for me every morning and to put me in good heart feed me little hot cakes with maple syrup up the road from my hotel. Personally, I have never cared much for pancakes at breakfast, but the late Mr Wiswell who conducted my affairs was never able to start a day without a massive pile of them, partaken at the counter. Once, driving back to await the phone call from the studio, he braked abruptly and stood or rather sat back while a gunman held up a garage. No shots were exchanged, only money passed hands. I was surprised at Mr Wiswell's refusal to be involved in the periphery of crime. He was the most correct man I ever met, everything about him, especially his hair, appeared to have been freshly laundered a half-hour earlier. He was punctilious to a fault. On the lot of MGM he extended courtesy until one feared it might snap altogether. Imagine my astonishment, therefore, when he seemed patently content not to interfere with highway robbery and we watched the action through the driving window and then drove off.

'Shouldn't we have done something?' I chided.

'No, I don't think so,' he replied, 'these garages usually carry a certain amount of insurance. Now, if Mr Mannix should call when I am not with you...' and he continued with the business of the day.

I learnt one thing about the American that morning: that he is not a man to be deterred. You cannot wave a gun or even your hat at him and distract his attention from the matter in hand. If he has decided to spend a morning operating an elevator it is useless to ask him to help do up or even transport a package. 'You need the Bell Captain,' he will tell you gravely, who will, alas, when you contact him, direct you to Dispatch.

Staying up country in Toronto recently I was appalled to find how far the American customer has drifted into becoming the American slave who will wait patiently for his master to allot him a bedroom, hand him his mail, seat him at table. Once in his own quarters he will be expected to leave them on a light signal and go downstairs for a message. Now he is the summoned.

Never ask for whom the light flickers, it flickers for thee.

Ah well, it was different when I first went to Hollywood or so I prefer to remember. There was a cosiness abroad, even Dave Chasen was there to welcome you. I often wonder who thought up the idea of a stand with the painted inscription 'Please wait to be shown to your table'.

'If you buy it,' the salesman told the proprietor, 'your customers will.' And so they have, and wait in patient queues before they are allowed to sit. When I was first in America no one had ever heard of a British queue; now, like the muffin, it has burst out all over.

In those days the Brown Derby was the place for titillation, the waitresses wore hooped skirts which meant there was a great deal less space for the customers who sat on the edge of their chairs watching the maidens stoop to deposit their trays. Perinos was the height of continental sophistication. I remember Hitchcock taking me and ordering the entire meal in French. I had no idea what to expect until the waiter bore down on us with the comestibles and enquired, 'Who gets the stuffed duck?' The best food was to be found at a club way out in the desert called The Dunes. Play started towards midnight and there was free champagne and the finest cold buffet this side of the Grand Canyon. Food was free too on the gambling boats moored at Santa Monica, but not so lavish, and there were beer counters along the strip which gave the stuff away along with the Splitz.

These were the days of the British Colony and there were a number of establishments vying for the patronage of C. Aubrey Smith and serving roast beef and steak and kidney pies however hot the weather might be. For myself the excitement of fresh strawberries mixed with the breakfast cereal, the corned beef hash and the apple pie *à la mode* made me resolve to become an American citizen as soon as possible. You have to go a long way now to find free food and even farther for corn beef hash. In later years when I made pictures in Los Angeles, I stay with my mother-in-law, Gladys Cooper, who preferred to cook for the family herself, having spent the whole day shopping in her Thunderbird. She would hurtle forty miles for Irish bread, which she fondly imagined had been baked the morning before on the banks of the Liffey. She would buy her honey in Culver City and parsnips at the Farmers' Market. Every now and then during the day there would be a screech of brakes, a flying figure would appear briefly at the pool edge, a door bang, a pound of butter be deposited in the refrigerator and she would take off once more, a great eagle swooping down Wiltshire and alighting briefly at the only ice-cream parlour in town where they made ginger and walnut fudge.

There is no doubt Gladys spoilt us for eating out, but very occasionally she would take us to her favourite restaurant, Trader Vic's. She always dreamt of settling finally on some remote Pacific island where she could pick and choose her own coconut.

The Doctor's Hat

It is now a great deal easier to visit China than it used to be, which is not to say I am any nearer to doing so. Only this last month I came across details of a holiday completely off the beaten Chinese track, a series of river excursions on all-purpose cargo paddle steamers that still ply on the great rivers of the central plateau. I confess to having made up the phrase 'central plateau' but, alas, I have lost the enticing brochure which contained all the details of such a rugged adventure. In any case I am supposed to be in Australia before long and China, unlike Java where I also haven't been as yet, never seems to be on the way to anywhere except itself. However, a small triumph has now been added to my travel trophy collection. I have crossed the Rocky Mountains by train. Always only an ambition until now, largely because I always seemed to be on the opposite side of Canada whenever I contemplated the journey and couldn't imagine what to do in Vancouver once I'd arrived there.

In point of fact there is not a great deal to do there, as I discovered when I flew from Los Angeles the other morning. By the time I had bought the ticket to Calgary, handed over the luggage to the Red Cap to be stowed in my parlour car and bought myself luncheon at the Four Seasons Hotel, I had time on my hands to spare as I wandered from bookshop to bookshop in search of some definitive guide to take on my great adventure. I searched in vain for some sort of background material. I wanted to know how long it took to build the line, how much it cost, how many Indians were slain and how many Chinese were crushed to death or fell from ice caps. I longed to read of the shanty towns which must have sprung up along the line, the gambling that went on, the bordellos which were closed down and how, for instance, the town of Medicine Hat came by its name.

I was to find out about the latter later but meanwhile I must in modesty recall that the only book which was actually pressed into my hand was my daughter-in-law's story of my life of which this particular bookseller was beginning to fear he might be overstocked. Egomaniac I may be, but I could not see myself seated in the observation car skimming such pages, and besides I already had a complimentary copy at home. In the end I had to content myself with the usual paperbacks of the detective stories of Ross Macdonald. I had, of course, read them all before but hope with Ross Macdonald burns eternal.

There are two trains a day across the mountains. Both seem to do most of the journey at night but I told myself there would still be several hours of daylight ahead and we might at least reach the foothills by dusk. I was, of course, wrong on both counts. I had pictured a thundering express hurtling along the track with a cowbell attached to warn the grizzlies that we were on our way. I found dilapidated aluminium commuter rolling stock with the smallest possible parlour in which my luggage took up every available space. Puffing and huffing I failed to observe a shelf on top of the partition which separated the compartment from the private loo and on which the Red Cap eventually stowed most of it when he made up the bed after dinner. There would, I told myself, be more room in the bar and taking with me a brochure of the Club Mediterranné, the sole literature provided, sought refuge behind a whisky sour and the company of the bar attendant as soon as the train started to crawl out of Vancouver. It continued to crawl for two hours except, as was often the case, when it stopped altogether. By dusk we had achieved the suburbs. We are not, I told the barman, going very fast and I wondered what could we be waiting for at such regular intervals.

'Freight,' he replied. 'Most of the line is single track.'

'This will take for ever,' I remarked, after my third whisky sour. 'How on earth can you hope ever to be in Montreal?'

'I don't hope to be in Montreal,' he told me, 'but you could be there sometime on Wednesday or it may be Thursday if you stay on the train, man.'

I told him I was getting off at Calgary.

'Me too,' he averred, 'and we shall be in Calgary by noon tomorrow.'

'Won't we be late?'

'No, we'll be on time.'

Obviously we were going to make up the hours we had squandered during the night. I pictured a track record as we hurtled along the track. I didn't seem able to forget the word hurtled. In point of fact the train never, as far as I could tell, approached thirty miles an hour on its entire journey. As most of the journey is accomplished through forests of Christmas trees laden with snow I suppose it is a wise precaution considering how close they grow to the track and the ever present risk of one falling on to it. I went back to my bedroom and confirmed my suspicion that nothing worked—there was no air-conditioning, no radio, no way of stopping up the basin but the lavatory was a shining exception. In point of fact there were individual lavatories to every compartment, indeed some seem to consist entirely of a single commode facing an upright chair. On the way to the dining-car I passed one room far larger than my own with a table stocked with bottles and a basket of flowers. I spent most of dinner trying to figure out to whom it belonged and decided it must be the woman who sat opposite me and who, it transpired, was herself a florist *en route* to Winnipeg to help her daughter in the same line of business with Christmas floral arrangements.

It seemed the train was her own Shangri La and she travelled on it whenever she could. 'I just can't wait to get on it,' she told me, 'it's so peaceful.' Her husband had been an inspector of accidents on the line. 'Reckon,' she observed, 'the CPR killed him, he just worked himself to death.' Not reassured by that statement I decided to switch to the Beaujolais to wash down the terrible chicken and suggested she might like to join me but she declined. I remembered the bottles and was not surprised: obviously a secret drinker, I told myself, as she volunteered another reason for travelling by train.

'I usually have one or two portraits with me in the luggage van.'

'What sort of portraits?' I asked.

'Commissioned portraits, I only paint on commission, I reckon art is something you have to be born with, I was fortunate,' she averred, 'and the money helps!'

'Tell me,' I pleaded, 'about Medicine Hat.'

'What about it? We shan't be there until tomorrow night. It's a nice enough little town, pity you won't see it in the dark.'

'I shan't see it at all,' I told her, 'I'm getting off at Calgary.' She seemed shocked at such a display of restlessness. Winnipeg, I gathered, was much further on. 'Why do you suppose it's called Medicine Hat?' I asked. By now we had been joined at the next table by the engineer, the assistant engineer, the inspector and head mechanic which roughly comprises the entire crew except there must be someone left in the cab to drive.

'It is called Medicine Hat,' one of them told me, 'because it was thereabouts the doctor lost his hat.'

'How?' I asked.

'It blew off into the brook, it's as simple as that.'

I don't know why I felt cheated but the sensation persisted when I arose at dawn or what ought to have been dawn to see the Rockies. Clouds and rain obscured them effectively all the way to Banff by which time the Rockies are slowing down like the train and levelling off. There wasn't a lot to see at Banff where all good Canadians go to ski. I guess I chose the wrong day. On the whole journey I never saw a living soul except outside Motor where two men stood beside the track snowballing each other while a third took pictures. The only thing I ever heard about Calgary was that the Prince of Wales before he met his Duchess once bought a ranch there and never went back, but I didn't mind leaving the train when we arrived and my luggage at the inevitable Four Seasons Hotel and riding to the top of the tower for luncheon and a view of the limitless plains of Alberta where now that the oil has become viable the boom is on. There is an excellent museum in Calgary showing how the railway was built with splendid photographs of the shanty towns and men and women straight out of Charlie Chaplin movies but I no longer cared.

I caught the plane to Montreal in a flurry of snow. 'Guess we are having our Indian summer,' the taxi-driver told me. 'Normally this time of the year it's real deep. Stays that way till June some years.' An elderly Dutchman, I asked him what had brought him so far afield, whether he didn't miss the clammy warmth of Holland. 'No,' he averred stoutly, 'Canada was the land of opportunity, particularly for children.'

'How many have you got?' I enquired.

'Three,' he replied, 'but they've all grown up now and gone back to Amsterdam with the grandchildren.'

If it wasn't for parents seeking new rearing grounds for their young, the airline business wouldn't be anything like as good as it is.

Meeting the President

The Edwardian Room at the Plaza commands an excellent view of the perspiring New Yorker hastening to his doom. Out of Central Park stream the new race of human lemmings intent on finding the cliff over which they must one day hurl themselves. Madness is in the air. Pollution forgotten, men, women and children in every stage of undress move rhythmically forward breathing in the carbon dioxide, propelled by the terror of growing old. Conversation has ceased—there is no breath left—the victims gulp and swerve through the traffic, ambulances parked at street corners advertise that they carry the latest in mobile life-support. The windows of the shops display running shoes, books on running, costumes for running, remedies for aching limbs, the newest in non-chafing lingerie, the ultimate in the jock strap. Nor is the scene indigenous to New York; in San Franscisco, on Nob Hill, the runners pause briefly to lift imagined weights and stand on tiptoe to conduct invisible orchestras. In Beverly Hills the populace is out on foot for the first time since they built Laurel Drive and Deep Water Canyon.

Running is recommended as the ultimate remedy for every ill that afflicts the race, from acne to constipation from incontinence to impotence. The gurus have abandoned the lotus position they once affected and now lead their followers on marathon races. Meditate On The Move is the new panacea. Knees Up For Uncle Sam, the universal motto. No longer does anyone in the States stand for public office, they needs must run for it. The newspapers, at least the ones which are still published, carry pages of advertisements urging their readers to enrol as students in running classes held hourly in hastily-rented stadiums and what would otherwise be empty polo fields and disused parking lots. The streets are paved with gold for anyone lucky enough to be in the business.

I withdrew my gaze from the window and regarded Mr Stuart Gottslea across the corned beef hash, a dish which is, alas, only procurable nowadays at breakfast when I seldom feel able to do it justice. Mr Gottslea was consulting his schedule; like me he had flown into New York the night before, preparatory to commencing our junket to promote *Too Many Chefs*, a film about to be released by Warner Brothers. Mr Gottslea had arrived from Los Angeles, I from Britain on the Concorde. There is no doubt that Concorde puts its stamp on a man; greatness is thrust upon him from the first moment he accepts the glass of champagne borne across the departure lounge by an English butler. 'Your champagne, sir,' he remarks, and we are reminded that this is the hour when we habitually accept a potion on a silver salver. Better still, it is the start of an adventure, an event so often missing these days from our lives; we are with the great ones at last, the toast is Lindbergh, or even the Wright Brothers coupled with Amy Mollinson and Monsieur Bleriot. The time taken for the flight is just three hours and ten minutes, far quicker apparently than a great shout can travel the air waves. We are confined, it is true—once the luncheon trolley is *en route* down the gangway, we must resist a sudden urge to wash our hands. No one complains. If only Charles Augustus could see us now, this is surely what he envisaged all those years ago.

Mr Heath claims his luggage at Kennedy a split second before I can do so with mine. There is no loss of face. Nice to see you on your own airline he tells me. Flogging a book I ask him? But this time apparently it is a speech in Chicago. He is born away in a limousine comparable to my own in which Mr Gottslea already waits.

Time to be off he warns now, as I scrape up the last mouthful of hash, we are starting with *Good Morning, Good Morning*.

Good Morning, Good Morning is a comparative newcomer to the breakfast table, the recognized and established leader is *Today, Today* but Miss Jacqueline Bisset, one of the stars of the picture, is taking care of that one.

In the collecting ring among the other guests eager to display their wares is an English lady who has written a book on fairies. I question her about a recent picture I had spotted in a newspaper of the little creatures snapped some years earlier by two little girls. True or false I enquired? They were manifestly pantomime fairies, she averred. There is a child star more composed than the rest of us and the producer of a television series on battered children, not physically, she told me, but mentally. Their parents don't speak to them. Too busy running, I observed sagely. The screen was showing an interview with the President, it was difficult to discover from the conversation what he was selling. The television producer came to a rather sticky end when she pleaded for another minute or so to put her case, the hostess cut her off in mid-flight in favour of a commercial advocating a new chewing gum guaranteed not to dislodge dentures, a dilemma I had never previously envisaged. If there is one thing we all have to learn on such occasions it is that you must never outstay your welcome—five or six minutes of stern interrogation in my case usually on how it feels to be fat and the screen is cleared to sell something really important. *Tomorrow, Tomorrow* is hosted by the usual immaculate lady with the lacquered hair and her companion, the all-purpose American male. Confidence and condescension earn them vast sums until their ratings fall. In marathon programmes lasting two hours every morning they conduct live but seldom lively interviews with at least a dozen diverse guests. A Trappist monk who has begun to speak again, a gangster who is suspected of kidnapping and murder, a doctor who has published a book on cloning, James Mason and/or Richard Harris. A singer with his heart on his new sleeve, Henry Fonda, Peter Ustinov. A man who claims to have made a fortune by simply writing chain letters. A husband and wife who have recently undergone simultaneous open heart surgery. The frenzy inside the studio is nicely matched by the activities of the viewers hastening to and from the bathroom gulping coffee, supervising the children's packed luncheons, wondering how they are going to pay the newly opened bills or whether the car will start.

Driving to work or the kids to school they will remember little they have seen and nothing of what they have heard except possibly that rain is predicted later.

To Day, To Day, recently deprived of the service of the legendary Miss Walters, has added a third host to the customary charismatic couple, a hatchet man who demolishes with undisguised gusto almost everything that has been staged, screened or written overnight. He is as near as America has come to recreating the late lamented George Kaufman—the gloom is there but not, alas, the wit.

Mr Gottslea has allotted the next hour for a photographic session which is accomplished in ten minutes flat by an obviously successful photographer fresh from snapping the late Pope and who stayed on for

His Holiness's funeral. An enthusiastic and friendly fellow who follows me down Fifth Avenue and across the Rockefeller Plaza recording my chance and all too brief meetings with his fellow countrymen who have flown or are contemplating flying British Airways and wish to apprise me of the fact. I wave and smile, pause for the occasional handshake and think how pleasantly extrovert must be the life of a campaigning senator.

Returning to the limousine we find our driver in confabulation with a traffic cop who is writing him out a ticket. Beside the cop lurks a gentleman who thrusts leaflets into our hands. These are short poems designed to help us over the worst of the ordeal with a message of Christian love and an admonishment to remember God is there to help in trouble. When the cop moves off the evangelist accompanies him in earnest conversation. It is difficult to decide which of them finds his task more congenial. I do my best to make Mr Gottslea's task congenial but fear I do not wholly succeed. Mr Gottslea is a company man, he plays for the side. Moreover, I gather he is not often allowed the treat of exercising the bulldog. He alternately strokes and chides, begging me to come to heel and not be late for the next encounter with the media. I am always a little late, I explain, that is the secret. The fear that I may have let the side down induces an entirely artificial euphoria when I show up. Get there on time or too early and they make you wait in the cloakroom. After ten days Mr Gottslea, his nerves shot to pieces, makes one final plea. By now we are in San Francisco. Please, please, he urges, tonight let us be on time, nay let us be five minutes before time for tonight you are to meet the president. Graciously I grant his request. If Mr Carter is going to take the trouble to come to yet another showing of the picture I shall certainly be there to receive him when he arrives. There is a moment of hesitation on Mr Gottslea's countenance; it is not Mr Carter who is expected apparently. For us there can be only one president. The President of Warner Brothers.

Late as I am that evening, the President is even later. He is wearing the best cut dinner jacket in the room. Slim, elegant and immensely weary, he portrays the Last Tycoon. Not since the late Sir Alexander Korda have I seen such a convincing performance of front office power. Mr Gottslea, positively quivering with emotion, indicates that I am to have an audience. I remember the warning of Alex's nephew, now the head of Simon and Schuster or very nearly, and himself the author of a book on where exactly to stand in the corridor of power. Against the wall, he advises, never move from the wall, let them come to you. Eventually the President came or at any rate passed. He said exactly the right thing, I said exactly the right thing. Mr Gottslea purred with joy. Wasn't that nice? he asked. My, wasn't that nice. Mr Gottslea found everything nice, the complimentary bottle of Scotch in the room or the bowls of fruit awaiting our arrival. The greeting of strangers on the side walks, the offer of coffee when we arrived at the studios, the view from the bedroom, above all each time his superior rang from the studio with a new assignment and the fond hope we were not getting too tired; his supreme ambition was to serve the organization.

Once, when I had opted out of a party and he had assured himself I was safely tucked up for the night, he hastened off to join in the revels. The next morning he was ecstatic; he had had, he told me, a wonderful time—the food was only moderate but he had managed to arrange an emergency plane booking for one of the vice presidents who had been obliged to return unexpectedly to base. The chief bone of contention between us was the telephone. There are men—and Mr Gottslea is one of them—who cannot bear to see a receiver rest on its cradle, he needs must take up the baby and play with it. When all else failed, he would ring his mother and urge me to say a few words to her. During the entire visit I resisted his admonition—for the life of me I cannot think why. It might well have, as he suggested, made her happy yet I stubbornly refused. I don't pretend Mr Gottslea brought out the worst in me, but he certainly didn't put it back. Yet I took considerable pains, as always, to project a pleasing image when confronted with camera or notebook, to express the gratitude all performers of my age genuinely feel in the continuing interest of the public as to what I eat, think and would like to alter in the world around me. I was kindness itself when discussing the making of the picture, exuberant in my praise of its director and my fellow players. Why then was I so beastly to Mr Gottslea? Now safely home again I can only hope he forgave me. Whether we were in New York, Los Angeles or San Francisco, my days followed a familiar pattern. Once I gave eighteen separate television interviews to far-flung correspondents brought in from Seattle, Boston, Cleveland, Dallas, San Antonio. They brought with them a roll of film, a clip board and a stop watch and always the same questions. The camera and I remained alone with a glass covered table on which rested sometimes a bottle of champagne, sometimes a pot of tea depending on their preference. We consumed a good deal of both while we chatted about Denver to where my first nurse retired or

Boston where my daughter-in-law's mother lives. I was urged to send personal messages to both. Nannie, alas, has been dead for half a century but I bravely complied. A lady who must have been almost my age recalled her grandson's gift to her on Mothering Sunday. A pair of running shoes. I put them on, she told me, and ran round the block. When I got home I received my first anonymous pornographic phone call. Maybe all they say about running is true after all.

Most evenings I was free to go to the theatre; it has been a wonderful season on Broadway. The city has regained its strength and courage. No longer do they boast of the muggings but of the thousands of tourists who have poured into New York since the dollar slumped, and the race of the tall ships and, surprisingly, the democratic convention alerted the United States citizen to the fact that in Manhattan, in the words of the song, there are 'nice people and the prices are right'. Not that they are all that right. The Palace Restaurant whither I was conducted to enjoy an early lunch with yet another TV host who has made a startling success in his role of Prairie Oyster (he once used to sing cowboy songs for his supper) costs just the eighty dollars before you've ordered the wine and a book currently going the rounds is entitled *New York on $500 a Day*. The cowboy who professed astonishment at a seven-course luncheon and didn't care for the mussel soup or indeed any of the fare was not an easy companion and seemed genuinely astonished at the inclusion of a sorbet between the remove and the roast. Whether he too was acting a part I couldn't determine; possibly both of us were more at home at Sardis where I shared a table with Harold Clurman, still presenting plays at over eighty and Richard Watts the dean of New York critics when I first hit the city in the early Thirties. I found the presence of both gentlemen reassuring. The biggest success in New York is a re-working of Conan Doyle's thriller *The Sign of Four*, retitled *The Crucifer of Blood*. A brilliant performance of Sherlock Holmes, scenes in an opium den, a storm which cost a hundred thousand dollars for the electronic thunder and lightning and the marvellous observation of the great detective that a one-legged sailor accompanied by a pigmy bent on mischief must have been noticed by someone, Watson! These days, of course, one cannot be so sanguine.

Life in Venice

Almost the first person we met in Venice was Jo Losey for whom, as usual, little was going right—a dejected lizard on the terrace of the Excelsior Hotel, not prepared to shed his tail for the benefit of the newshounds.

'You'll feel better now,' my daughter-in-law told me, when several of them had angled their shutters to include myself. 'You know how you like having your photograph taken on holiday. You don't have to give them your name each time, all they are asking is that you keep your mouth shut. They are perfectly capable of finding out who you are later.'

'I wouldn't count on it,' said Jo. 'The rooms here are far too small and I don't care much for the food, added to which I cannot find out to whom I am supposed to lecture and when. It isn't a well-organized film festival at all.'

'It isn't exactly a festival,' Sheridan told him. 'More of a dry run for next year.' My son, like myself, has always believed it possible to teach a grandmother to suck eggs.

'Whatever it is,' said Jo, 'I shouldn't be here. I am still cutting *Carmen*. He may have said *Rigoletto*. I have never been much of a listener and anyway when I am with Jo I like to hear him grumble.

'A good journey?' I enquired hopefully.

'Terrible,' Jo told me, and we left him and his always cheerful wife and took the grandchildren to the beach restaurant to gorge on the antipasta. Years ago we used to bring their parents to the Lido so they could see Gregory Peck and Gina Lollobrigida; my family don't go much for ancient monuments unless they happen to be in show-biz. Culture, I used to tell myself, will come later.

We weren't staying at the Excelsior, but further along the beach at

Hotel Des Bains which now has added a beautiful swimming pool to its amenities but I still prefer to laze under striped awnings in front of their *cabanas* on the sea shore. After the wine and the crayfish and the photographers my family thought we should stroll back.

'That's Bogdanovich,' they told each other as we stepped over him and prevailed on Hugo, my most outgoing grandchild, to demand his autograph. 'If he signs it correctly,' we told him, 'ask for six tickets to his film showing.'

He returned in triumph. 'He'll send them on,' he told us. Later we discovered the children weren't allowed in and Hugo took his contemporaries to the amusement arcade instead. The amusement arcade is open quite late and the discothèque by the pool never seemed to close. I suppose it's good for children to stay up till all hours; they have to get used to it sooner or later, and the three-year-old usually took a nap in the afternoons.

There were, of course, other cultural treats in store. Luncheon at Torcello where Monica Vitti sat at the next table, and once again Hugo settled the argument and brought back the spoils though he found it difficult to explain to her how to write his name. 'I don't think many Italians call their children Hugo,' he remarked. In Murano I swept some rather delicate glass bird off the show table and had to proffer my American Express card to mollify the proprietors. Still I got the rest of the loot safely home without breakage along with my exquisite shell box from which I had previously evicted my remaining cigars and then had to bathe rather more often than I had planned to wash the glue from my fingers.

One Sunday we sat on the terrace of the Gritti Palace to watch the Regatta. At first, as elderly ladies rowed up and down paddling furiously, we thought it would never start. The winners of previous years are allowed a victory lap. I estimated some of the veterans had participated in events prior to the last war. The ceremonial processions with a real-life costumed Doge impressed even the three-year-old. Espying the television cameras, she was a mite disappointed to find no one actually fell into the Grand Canal, convinced she was watching yet another edition of that perpetual European favourite, *It's a Knock Out*.

'Shouldn't we be further down stream?' she enquired, 'where the real fun begins?' 'You can't move till seven o'clock,' we had to tell her, and plied her with complimentary glasses of champagne and peaches. Luckily she preferred Coca-Cola.

One of the great advantages of family holidays is that one of us is always available to polish off the spare pasta and Bellinis.

We kept promising the children we would find the restaurant where the man came round after dinner with the mechanical toys and had them rushing between the coffee cups. Bears with drums, somersaulting monkeys, Italian terriers lifting their legs, and the rabbit which fed itself a carrot. We still have the rabbit from twenty years ago, without the carrot, alas. We found the trattoria but the man never showed. Dead, the proprietor told us sadly, and the son never managed to keep the plates spinning all at the same time and finally packed up. The *carabinieri* with their plumed helmets no longer parade in pairs and tourists hell-bent on walking between them have to content themselves like the late Diaghilev with never walking between the two great flagpoles on the Quay by the Vaporettos if they want to come back here. For myself, I always want to come back to Venice. There is nowhere else in the world where people seem to have more fun. Where else but in St. Mark's Square would the city fathers erect a gigantic screen and show Lillian Gish in *Broken Blossoms* backed by a full orchestra, or stage a retrospective exhibition of that most reckless of all war photographers, the late Mr Cappa? Past the casino and the last hotel at the very tip of the Lido, long after the promenade has ended and where the mosquitoes make the last stand, is the Murazzi, built over the ancient white stone fortifications from which it takes its name. A wooden chalet on the edge of nowhere, but where the ferry very occasionally runs to the Island of St. Peter Caught on the Hop, if my Italian serves, and serve it must. Here you eat the best sea food I have ever tasted. Even the squid is no longer made of indiarubber.

PENMANSHIP

All My Own Words

Life can be full of disappointments or delightful surprises. It depends on how high you set your sights. A bottle of wine is either half empty or half full.

If there is one thing I have learnt the hard way it is not to expect to sell one of my books over the counter. I have, like most authors, occasionally found myself, fountain pen at the ready, poised before a table optimistically piled with one or sometimes several of my masterpieces. After an hour or two, often the pile seems to have grown. On the rare occasions when someone puts down the money and gives me the book to sign, I am overwhelmed with gratitude.

'To whom shall I make it out?' I enquire for all the world as if I was about to hand the recipient a blank cheque or at least a substantial postal order.

'To my Aunt Dora,' comes the riposte; people seldom seem to buy my books to read themselves. Gleefully I sign with a flourish and then sit back and wait twenty minutes or so for the next customer. Of course it is not all inactivity, often quite busy people will come in and ask for a reliable book on bee-keeping or enquire where the blotting paper is for sale. They tend to ignore the outsize poster advertising my coming or if they do see it, avert their eyes as if someone were thrusting a collecting box under their noses.

Publishers never give up and, luckily I suppose for us, neither do bookshop owners and just occasionally they strike gold but not with me, alas. Just as some actors can cause a queue to form at the stage door to watch their favourites leave the fray or indeed sometimes even arrive for it, so other authors do occasionally attract the crowds. Edward Heath when he gave up the country and took to the sea, sold hundreds of thousands of books about sailing. People who had resented his hand on the tiller of state went mad about his reminiscences tossing about in the Solent. They even took him around in a train and people queued on the platform to spend five guineas and have their copy autographed by the jolly tar himself.

At least I was once praised for having an altogether more gracious manner when scrawling my name on the fly leaves. 'You always,' said Mr Heffer who runs not one but at least seven bookshops in Cambridge, 'you always take time out to hope they will enjoy the work.' Mr Heath merely grunted but then, of course, he was under considerably greater pressure. Indeed, at his peak he was reputed to sign a thousand an hour. Of course I am sure I could have topped him, it was just that I was never asked to do so. Ten an hour and I am glowing with pride and profit. Once in Richmond, Virginia, where business seemed more than ordinarily slack, I pursued the customers into the neighbouring electrical department. 'Before you put your money down for that refrigerator, madam,' I told one matron, 'consider whether you shouldn't buy my book.'

She turned a startled eye in my direction. 'I think I should warn you, whoever you are, that I am with my husband,' she told me. Richmond, Virginia, *papparazzi* never willingly photograph a man holding a glass of liquor in his hand, and I withdrew in some disorder mindful that such bold tactics might get me arrested in these parts for attempted rape. Authors are often among the more timid of *Homo sapiens* and few beside myself actually relish the moment when they guest on the chat shows or are cajoled into a signing session or a literary luncheon when they are expected to say a few words preparatory to selling a few books. It is a formidable task and by the time the customers have paid for the luncheon, few have change in their pockets to invest in a hardback at £7 and upwards. My daughter-in-law, having published a biography of myself and there is surely no harm here in mentioning a title so apposite and revealing as *Larger Than Life*, we recently accepted with alacrity an invitation to present ourselves at a bookshop in Henley-on-Thames and be prepared for vigorous and sustained calligraphy.

'Henley,' I assured her, 'will be a piece of cake.' In so far as I have a home town, this is the one I have lived only a few miles away from for more than forty years. I once owned a kindergarten school here; my mother-in-law dwelt on the Regatta Reach; I am familiar, if not on speaking terms, with a thousand faces. For nearly half a century I have waited in car parks while the family shopped, have patronized the local dentist, queued up with the grandchildren at the local cinema for holiday showings of *Jaws*. I remember the town when it had the best pastry cooks in Britain and the High Street before it went one way.

I have taken hazardous voyages along the Thames, steered by the children and grandchildren, argued with the lock-keeper and traffic wardens, signed petitions to resite the War Memorial, watched amateur acting and given prizes for gondola races. I even took the great Jack Paar himself to the local grammar school and filmed the children playing tennis without the encumbrance of tennis balls. Inasmuch as anywhere belongs to me and I to it, Henley is my sort of town. So it was with a heart filled with optimism and a breast pocket with biros, that I made my way at eleven o'clock precisely to rendezvous with booklovers of Henley and the surrounding district.

The bookshop had thoughtfully provided three separate tables and a bottle of champagne. On previous occasions in the district I have found it wiser to announce beforehand that free champagne would be available not only for myself but for any bona fide customer or personal friend. Perhaps this was the mistake we all made on this occasion, at any rate I was amazed to find the premises comparatively deserted. Indeed, if it hadn't been for the staff who clustered bravely around to have their picture taken by the sole photographer, our publisher, who had thoughtfully brought his small daughters who had been promised a barbecue and a swim, and my own grandchildren who fortunately had some of their school friends staying for the weekend, we would have been hard put to it to muster what Genghis Khan used to call a horde.

I don't say the public didn't show up later, although scarcely in the numbers anticipated, but if anything sold that morning I should have said it was Paddington Bear. It's quite extraordinary what children read these days. Still I did manage to sign a few of those and one benefactor actually bought one of all our copies on display but he turned out to be a friend of the publisher. All in all, if it hadn't been for the champagne, it might have proved a sobering experience. Why was it, asked my grandson a few hours later, clutching a burnt sausage as he dried himself in the sun, that no one came?

It's all in the Bible, I told him sadly. A prophet is not without honour save in his own country and in his own house.

'We honour you, Pa,' he comforted me. 'Have a banger.'

Dressing to Kill

It is a great help to a man to be in love with himself. For an actor it is absolutely essential. Self love is the most enduring and satisfactory emotion of which human life is capable. I have little patience with anyone who is not self-satisfied. I am always pleased to see my friends, happy to be with my wife and family, but the high spot of every day is when I first catch a glimpse of myself in the shaving mirror. At the same time I am aware that my fans and I cannot always continue to grow old together. Some of them must, alas, fall by the wayside or grow too old and infirm to totter down the aisle even at matinées. They must, of necessity, content themselves with their memories of my performances in earlier and happier days. My problem, therefore, since memory pays nothing at the box office, is to entrap others who have so far evaded the net which I have so assiduously cast in the small pond of which I own the fishing rights. I have never been a deep sea fisherman: it is not in my nature to trawl in the vast oceans where Olivier, Richardson, Gielgud and Jason Robards defy the elements. I avoid the great play as I would the great wave. I prefer the ripples of laughter, and when I am becalmed or capsized I have only to step from the boat and wade ashore.

Enough of metaphors: the problem which faces me these days is to find a role for a septuagenarian who isn't either a mad scientist or a heart-broken academician or a gin-soused old circus clown, or even an octogenarian butler who dies mysteriously in Act I.

I have a lifelong friend—and I sometimes wonder how we have mutually sustained the relationship—who directs meaningful plays by little-known Bulgarians (little known, of course, outside Bulgaria) and who descends on me whenever I am out of work bearing a play he is about to direct for some worthy but obscure provincial festival with the serious intention of transferring it later to Shaftesbury Avenue when all the contracts can be renegotiated, and urges me to read it forthwith. 'It is not the sort of part you usually play,' he informs me, 'but it has one wonderful scene when you are under a motor car trying to change a tyre. We never see your face but it would be a splendid chance to act with your feet, to really act, you understand. I know you could do it if only you would give yourself a chance.'

'I like to show my face,' I tell him. 'Furthermore, I like it to be seen right through the play and I like to be standing upright or, better still, sitting down centre stage.'

'Oh, well,' he tells me as he drives off after luncheon, 'at least I've tried to get you to act properly. But if you won't, you won't.'

'I won't,' I shout to him as he turns out of the drive, 'and I never will.'

I have, however, struck a new and promising seam in the hut at the bottom of the garden where I habitually write my plays, or rewrite the works of others. A man called John Wells, a fellow contributor to *Punch* (where fortunately my son Sheridan occupies an editorial chair) who has even written for *Private Eye* and was once a master at Eton College, arrived with clean paper and carbons and his own typewriter and, insisting that I should sit in the armchair while he pounded away at my desk, managed to get down in four days three acts of a play which had been flitting around aimlessly in my head for months. Little did I dream when we finished *A Picture of Innocence* and tried it out for two weeks in Britain before taking it to Toronto, that it was to attract the sort of fish I always suspected swam in my pond but hitherto had lurked inconspicuously in the darker waters of despondency.

The play is about transvestism, the tale of three happily, or fairly happily, married men, two of whom have kept their wives in ignorance of their compulsive hobby. It is my determination that all should share our secret that leads at least for a time to unlooked-for complications, and a fairly disastrous tea party. It is, of course, a very English play.

A play about transvestites does not necessarily attract transvestites to pay to come and see it. It is the greatest theatrical fallacy that because, for instance, the world is mad about football or golf you have only to construct a third act in the goal mouth or on the eighteenth tee to have the theatre filled with hearty kickers or happy putters. They usually stay away happily kicking or putting till the sun has gone down and the curtain risen.

Imagine my delight, therefore, when even before the rehearsals started, we were contacted by one of the founder members of the Beaumont Society which exists to see that any transvestite who joins shall in future be a happy transvestite and not be tempted as is, alas, sometimes the case, to despair of his hobby, to dress himself up for the last time in his wife's petticoats and await her return one summer evening hanging from the bannisters. There is no need, the society urges its members, for drastic action, and it is always a mistake to wear your wife's petticoat – you will inevitably stretch it.

While the play was turning over in my mind I visited my younger son in Australia, partly to reassure myself that his new home was fully carpeted, partly to extol Mr Heinz's soups which I have been doing now for almost as long as I have been urging the Americans to fly British Airways. My dream is of one day combining the two performances. It's curious how advertisers are so reluctant to get together and have, for instance, Rex Harrison selling a Rolls Royce to David Niven over a cup of coffee. It is something I hope to achieve in the future, for I am a man of boundless ambition. However, to get back to my son who is a theatrical impresario in the Antipodes and had recently put on a play with Gordon Chater entitled *Elocution of Benjamin Franklin* which deals with an elocution teacher who brings down the wrath of Melbourne – or just possibly Sydney – on his head by venturing forth in drag and being wrongly accused of child molestation. Transvestites, as far as I know, never molest anyone and the play, as all good plays should, sends the audience home to ponder man's inhumanity to man.

In the course of rehearsals, my son, altogether more painstaking than his father, had had the benefit of advice from the Sea Horse Club. The Sea Horse Club is a world-wide organization with roughly the same high purpose as the Beaumont Society and it was arranged that I should entertain the club's secretary to dinner. He came, of course, *en femme* and my initial reaction was one of embarrassment. For one thing I felt he was not wearing the right wig, for another I felt qualms about venturing into the hotel restaurant with a lady who so patently was not quite what she seemed. I had Mr Heinz's reputation to consider besides my own. Now six months later and knowing a great deal more, I marvel at my cowardice. Only today, trying on a new wig in Harrods, it seemed perfectly natural to be discussing the best way to avoid appearing not only as a transvestite but as mutton dressed as lamb. It is a trap most of us fall into. Petrina, the secretary, had told me over dinner in my sitting-room, 'Be careful to look your age, or,' she added kindly, 'perhaps in your case, not quite your age.'

Petrina, I found, had no real desire to be mistaken for a woman. 'Does the waiter suspect?' I asked her when he had retired after serving the smoked salmon.

'He'd be a fool if he didn't,' she replied. 'I talk like a man.'

'Then what on earth is the object of it all?' I asked.

'I am not sure there is an object,' she told me, 'it's just that dressed as a woman we all feel more relaxed, more comfortable than we do in business suits.'

Petrina, or Peter as she is called by day, belongs to the dreaded profession of business efficiency experts who follow executives around their offices with a stop watch noting their potential for time-wasting while on the job. 'As a rule,' she remarked, 'we are a ruthless crowd; if you can avoid doing business with us it is, on the whole, better to do so for we usually get the better of you.'

As Petrina, however, she seemed to have a heart of gold and cared deeply for the plight of those who felt themselves cut off and lonely. Some men, she told me, will take a room at a motel for the night and just dress themselves up and sit alone staring into a mirror not daring to telephone room service. Then in the morning they will bundle up their dresses and make-up and throw them out of the car or hand them over to the Red Cross vowing never again to give in to their other personality. Of course, it never works. A month later they are shopping around frantically. In time they learn economy, if never courage.

'Can you learn courage?' I asked.

'If you belong to the Sea Horse Club we try and give you courage; we insist, for instance, that new members shall attend in costume and not sneak in and try and change on the premises. To go out *en femme* is the supreme release.'

'When they arrive do you compliment them on their dress?'

'No, not often. We usually criticize each other if we discuss each other at all but usually we are more interested in asking them how we look.'

'Do you wish to attract men?'

She found that a difficult one to answer. 'I am not homosexual but I like men to think how well I wear my clothes. But it's really people I know that afford me the most satisfaction. If, for instance, I am in the supermarket I am delighted if one of my neighbours who knows me as both Peter and Petrina tells me how nice I look. The neighbours matter to me.'

'What about your children?'

'They still call me Father. I would like them to call me Petrina like my wife does when I am dressed, but they never remember. I don't think children should be nagged.'

'The other day,' Petrina went on, 'I thought it might be nice to open a separate bank account I could charge my clothes to. A lot of the stores have special departments for our lot.

'I went along to my bank manager and explained I wanted to open a separate account for her. He thought at first I was talking about my girl friend.'

'And when he found out?' I asked her, thinking that an Australian bank manager might have suggested she took both accounts elsewhere.

'He invited me to the rugby club of which he is secretary; he thought his members ought to know about it.'

It was an unexpected reaction, but by now I am used to those. Waiting at the stage door the other afternoon I found an elderly gentleman who had seen the play. 'I enjoyed it very much, you got nearly all of it right. You are, of course, a fellow transvestite?' I told him I was only pretending. 'I am,' he went on, 'a retired bank manager. Of course in my job I had to be discreet and then again my wife was never very keen on the idea. Do wait till I'm dead, she used to beg me and now she is and I am very lonely. As you get older it seems sadder but I thought I must cheer myself up before coming to see you, so I went shopping; something I haven't done for months.'

'What did you buy?' I enquired.

'Not much at all, talcum powder and a very expensive petticoat.'

We rehearsed our play in petticoats, at least the men did. Not expensive ones, but just to get the feel. The play is a comedy, everything comes right in the end. I wouldn't wish it otherwise.

I am not a great one for hobbies. I play no game in the open air, am not attracted to camping in the high Alps or canoeing over Niagara Falls, nor have I been able to listen with very much enthusiasm as my friends recount their experiences in and around golf or cricket clubs. But I can understand a man collecting teddy bears or letters written by soldiers about to die in the Boer war; I can even understand why a friend of my youth used to strip himself to the buff before donning a mackintosh and venturing forth to his friendly neighbourhood drug store, only to whip the wrapping away before the startled gaze of the young lady behind the prescription counter. It had to be her, of course. He was usually beaten up by irate bystanders, often arrested, fined and once imprisoned, but his compulsion continued through the years. 'Does it still persist?' I asked, meeting him only the other day at a luncheon party.

'Alas no,' he told me. 'What would be the use? The most excitement I could expect would be to be tapped on the shoulder by the lady behind me in the queue and urged to move over as *she* hadn't got all day to waste!'

We are, I suppose, sobering up as the great earth on which we live does the same. In the years to come, indeed, it may be impossible to dress distinctively as a member of either sex but meanwhile transvestites play happily in the short time that remains to them. They sit before the tea table on their 'at home' evenings much as my grandmother used to do awaiting the callers, always announced by three discreet rings on the doorbell. Less than that they don't answer, at least until they've disrobed and unwigged. There would be too much explaining to do, for although there are three transvestites in every thousand, the odds are still against the milkman and to a slightly lesser degree, the clergy being of like mind.

'I had one,' a successful bishop told me after he'd seen the play. 'He would wear ladies' camiknickers under his vestment and was highly excited on the occasion of a service attended by Royalty. "If only she'd known I was wearing my frillies," he kept remarking afterwards, "what do you suppose she would have said?" "Nothing," I told him. "Royalty make it a habit to say nothing on such occasions." All the same I watched him pretty carefully next time.'

What might shock the faithful luckily seldom affronts the theatre-goer who, from Terence's time, has delighted in the joke of men pretending to be women or better still, eunuchs. I made a few mistakes initially with the play, expecting the audience to relish more a scene lifted from *Charley's Aunt*. I hadn't realized, I suppose, that the dilemma of Auntie is a trifle more hair-raising; but now that I take to filling my handbag with celery sticks the laughs come more freely. The public I find gets used to everything, even to the fact that I have thicker ankles than I would wish these days. But I don't think once my role is finished in *A Picture of Innocence*, I shall continue to primp and preen. For one thing, it takes an unconscionable time to get dressed.

Easy Reader

When the bidding for the bay colt by Habitat out of Word from Lundy and therefore a half-brother of the great Grundy himself reached forty thousand guineas, my neighbour who had shown no inclination to partake in the Houghton Sales up to then agitated his catalogue. By the time he was established among the competitors the price had reached sixty thousand, around ninety he dropped out of the auction. I am not sure what the final price was, all I know was Mr Sangster secured the prize. Mr Sangster usually gets what he wants, so for that matter does Mr Abdullah, who earlier in the evening had paid two hundred and forty-odd thousand for a two-year-old whose pedigree escapes me but obviously impressed Mr Humphrey Cotteril who bought it on his behalf. Humphrey is an old friend with a distinguished career on the turf now, alas, behind him. To spend two hundred and forty thousand pounds of someone else's money did not daunt him, but he did opine wistfully that life might have been just as easy for him had Mr Abdullah appeared earlier on the scene when he was training them himself. Mr Abdullah is manifestly the sort of owner to have. As for my neighbour, he wasn't bidding for himself either but on behalf of the Irish National Stud. Ran out of petrol, was how he described the encounter. 'You couldn't have stalled at a better moment,' I told him. In four days at Newmarket only interrupted by the races themselves, Tattersalls managed to get through close on ten million of other people's money. While the colts and fillies remain wonderfully calm as they parade under the spotlights, the putative owners plunge and occasionally swear quite loudly when thwarted of the spoils.

The auctioneer adopts the stance of a drill sergeant with the awkward squad. Make no mistake, he tells his listeners, it's against you in the gate. I am selling, make no mistake, put her in at fifteen, she is bound to make more, make no mistake. All right then, five, three, who'll give me two thousand, start where you like, he concedes, a shade ungraciously. You won't want to lose her, he insists, eyeing the last bidder but one three minutes later and urging further extravagance. Make no mistake, sixty thousand for the Derring Do filly. I am giving her away, shall I say seventy? By far the most dignified of all is the gentleman who follows hard on the heels of yearlings sweeping up their droppings into neat piles and removing what must surely be the most precious fertilizer in the world. I have no idea what he gets paid but then of course, he is not Grundy.

Earlier, I had stood at the bar talking to Mr Doyle himself, the most famous of all the dealers, and remembering the time when I had myself bought a little filly at those same sales for just £200 and who had subsequently won me four races before setting sail for Australia with my blessing while a cheque for £6,000 nestled in my pocket. But those days have gone for ever – just as well, perhaps, or the breeders would have gone too. Something of an innocent abroad, I have admired a son of Brigadier Gerard being paraded outside the ring. You are not, I hope, thinking of buying that one, a soft Irish voice chided in the dusk. I might, I lied. You'll get him cheap enough, they won't bid for him. Why not? I asked. He's sixteen hands already, you'd have to cut him and put him away for jumping.

I made my way into the sale ring, a plan to win the Grand National in 1985 already forming in my mind. He pricked up his ears in the ring, so did I. I grasped my catalogue firmly, even practising a surreptitious wave. He fetched twelve thousand. Someone didn't know what he was talking about. Could it have been me?

The next morning I repaired to Cambridge where it had been arranged I should follow in Mr Heath's footsteps and sign copies of my new book. At £3.50 we were obviously giving it away. Make no mistake, I told my first customer, I am selling. The bidding, though brisk by bookshop standards, was not a patch on Tattersalls. I managed a couple of hundred in an hour or so and received a nice compliment from an *aficionado*. 'You are much nicer to them than Mr Heath, he seldom looked up. Mind you there isn't quite the pressure in your case.'

I looked up once to find Professor Glyn Daniel who with the late Mortimer Wheeler once had the most successful panel game on the box. He was still blaming Mrs Wyndham Goldie for taking it off and so, come to think of it, am I.

Lunch with the publishers was memorable for a superb raspberry Pavlova and the extraordinary numbers of Heffers around the Board. But then, of course, they have nine bookshops in Cambridge. I was determined to show my appreciation for the efforts all had been making to sell the book and to get away in time to see the Dewhurst Stakes run. The difference between publishing and the racing world is largely a matter of confidence. The chips are fairly heavily loaded against success but racing people are mercifully unaware of it.

Meeting Mr Charles Benson in the Members' Enclosure amply rewarded me for not lingering over the coffee. 'I have only three things to say to you,' he told me, 'and you had better write them down.' I can gratefully record that they all won.

The pace in Suffolk is quickening all the time. I put up at Clare which now boasts two excellent hotels and shares with Long Melford up the road the tourist trade disembarking at Harwich, mostly Dutch apparently, inspecting Constable country, Ely Cathedral and Ipswich. Do they go to *Hedda Gabler*? I asked in astonishment, noticing a bill advertising the performances. Some of them are Norwegian, the landlord explained. The crush was such that I had to keep changing hotels, spending one night in the erstwhile home of C.P. Snow on the banks of the Stour and now an inn famous for its breakfasts.

I had an uncle once who lived nearby in a moated grange and reportedly loved Mrs Belloc Lowndes. I don't remember whether he ever asked me to visit him there but he used sometimes to send my mother postcards with a picture of his home. I thought it might be nice to find it again. In the sunshine Giffords, as it was called, looked even lovelier than it did on a postcard. Mrs Belloc Lowndes was the most successful woman novelist of the day. Who then was Mr Belloc Lowndes you may ask? Not, alas, my uncle who would have liked to have been. I let down the window and accosted an elderly retainer.

'Anyone home?' I enquired.

'No, Mr Gardener is away.'

'My uncle lived here once,' I told him. We turned the car and drove off, I didn't want him to think I was a burglar doing a reconnaisance. Nor must I give the impression that my Uncle Dolph was a sort of late Edwardian Heathcliff wandering disconsolately around Constable country shouting Mrs Belloc at the top of his voice.

Suffolk is, after all, a very different part of the world, and the pace here is altogether softer. As it says in the guide book, it is a part of

England where the pace of life is remarkably slow and restful and people have time to bid you good-day—and good morning, of course.

TREADING THE BOARDS

My Public

There are actors who shrink from recognition, playing a perpetual game of hide-and-seek. Alec Guinness, Paul Scofield, Elizabeth Taylor. No one, I told the latter, will know you in Leningrad; put a scarf over your hair and come for a walk, or come downstairs and dine with me in the hotel restaurant. The Russians stood on their chairs to get a better view. Miss Taylor ate very little.

No one has ever stood on a chair to see me. If there is any chance of my not being recognized, I stand on the chair. For everyone who can put a name to the face there are ten who can't. These are the ones who ask for autographs; mine is not the most legible signature, especially when scrawled on a newspaper in pencil. I leave them to puzzle it out. Some prefer to continue guessing, and expect me to halt until they have succeeded. 'Don't tell me,' they will urge, 'I'll be there in a moment.'

'I have to be there sooner than that,' I reply, 'the name is Morley.'

'That's right,' they tell me, 'Christopher Morley,' and we part friends.

Not all my colleagues enjoy such interruptions; they have other and more serious purposes in life than being quizzed or being told by strangers that the last time he or she met them was on a plane bound for Jersey fifteen years ago. 'I don't suppose you'll remember,' they add for further identification, 'they were plumb out of gin.' It is, of course, always impossible to recall the incident, but I for one go on my way sustained by the hope that we shall meet again fifteen years from now and one of us be sufficiently impressed to recall our second meeting.

Only on race courses do I refuse to autograph. Alastair Sim, among others, always refused to give them. He would explain, at considerable length, his objections to such a foolish request. He refused to litter the world with idiotic scraps of paper. Nowadays his signature is valuable. For some reason the Germans and the Americans are the most avid autograph collectors. They write from Bremen and Minnesota in facsimile enclosing international tokens and a half-dozen blank sheets. I never sign more than one; if, as one supposes, the sender is commercially orientated one doesn't want to flood the market.

Now and again you will be shaken by the hand by someone who knows your brother in Orpington. The fact that to the best of your knowledge you haven't a brother carries little weight on such occasions. The stranger departs, convinced you are lying and that you are estranged from your relative. You depart wondering if (as in the case of a theatrical friend) your father kept the existence of an entirely separate brood a secret. My friend was tempted to investigate further the chance remark of a bookseller, and discovered he had not one but several brothers and sisters or, more correctly, half-brothers and sisters. But in my case I have been content to let sleeping dogs lie.

Occasionally I get dead rats and even more unpleasant anonymous gifts through the post. I tell myself that it is unlikely that the former were contaminated by plague, and that I have reduced the intolerable pressure of some fellow lunatic. I refuse to accept it as a judgement on my performance. The older one grows the more pleased are one's contemporaries to see one, although not necessarily performing in the theatre. They are heartened by such encounters. There is a strong geriatric bond. Some recall how well one looks; others, an occasion many years ago when they first caught sight of one across the footlights. They strive to remember the name of the piece, or the date, or where they were at the time. It is often a slow process of gradual recall. One hesitates to prompt, even if one could. The parting is delayed but pleasurable. They go on their way remembering something entirely different. How fond they were of Aunt Maud who provided the matinée treat. One is left with the name of the leading lady on the tip of the tongue.

Americans make the best fans, perhaps because they always seem to have time on their hands. The native young pound along behind, thrust a cigarette packet into one's hand, and are off back to the shop. Worst of all are the temporarily incapacitated who demand you sign the plaster on the fractured limb. I find it well nigh impossible to scratch on plaster of Paris, yet others seem to manage.

Few ask for themselves; it is usually for a child. 'My little granddaughter will be so excited,' they urge, but surely a candy bar or a toy is a more suitable present? I can hardly bear to contemplate the disappointment. 'Guess what grandpa has for you?' The small victim searching the pocket and coming up with a squashed plastic cup bearing the signature of someone of whom she is totally ignorant. 'Don't cry, dear, and Grandpa will go out right away and bring back an iced lolly.'

New Zealanders often produce passports; there is a certain satisfaction in writing on an official document. The suspicion that in so doing I may have invalidated it doesn't seem to occur to them, as it does to me. I should, I suppose, be grateful that at least people don't seem to want to write their names on me, as they do on other ancient monuments—and I am.

Heavier citizens demand that I should follow them, to be introduced to their wives on the grounds that the latter often remark on our striking resemblance. Functioning as I do as a sort of decoy duck for British Airways, I am hailed as a friendly counsellor whose advice has been accepted, and on other occasions blamed for delays at Heathrow. Sometimes asked if I ever resent being better known for performances in television advertisements than as the definitive Hamlet of my time, no, I tell them bravely, in the world of commercials everything ends happily and that is precisely what I aim to do.

Of course, it has not been so easy for the children, and now the grandchildren, who are at times appalled by my constant *bonhomie*. My son once summed it all up. 'There are times, Papa, when you made us cringe a little, but taking it by and large we got the service.'

My Critics

I learnt my trade in the twenty years between the great wars and immediately following the last one and, whether I like it or not, am now an old dog who fails to learn new tricks. New tricks were frowned on in those days. The theatre was somewhere for the pleasure seeker to rest between dinner and an evening on the town. It was the stalls that mattered; without them life was just not possible.

The stalls put on dinner jackets and picked up their tickets at the box office. These had been reserved for them by the ticket-agency libraries like Keith Prowse and it was on the advice of the librarians that we both depended.

There were, in those days, critics of considerable reputation such as Morgan on *The Times*, St John Ervine on the *Observer*, Agate on the *Sunday Times* and even Hannen Swaffer who wrote for the *Express*. Like the monarch, their function was to advise and warn and they often succeeded in being extravagantly witty and amusing at the expense of the playwright or the cast, but the real power of life and death was vested in a mysterious and comparatively anonymous Mr Smith, who, although nominally only the buyer for Keith Prowse, also largely influenced the attitude of his colleagues who represented a number of smaller firms whose names, with the exception of Lacon and Ollier and Ashton Mitchell, I have, alas, forgotten.

It was Mr Smith who decided whether the libraries would do the deal.

If he approved, he waited on the manager the next morning and guaranteed to sell enough stalls to keep the attraction running for three, six and sometimes twelve months ahead. Although Mr Smith was not available to customers, Miss Parker, who was in charge of the ticket counter at Ashton Mitchell, became a close friend of mine and I used to drop in on her establishment in Bond Street to chat her up, as the saying goes these days.

Miss Parker's customers were the *crème de la crème*. It was she who decided how they should spend their evenings during the season, or when they were perforce up from the shires in the winter because frost suspended hunting, or unexpectedly at a loose end after Goodwood week, or simply staying at Claridges for Christmas shopping. When she booked them boxes at Ascot or centre court seats at Wimbledon, she would urge that they also took in The Hippodrome or His Majesty's later in the day. It wasn't necessary for her to describe or even name the play. All they had to be told was the venue and starting time so that they could instruct their chauffeurs.

Some names were familiar: Nares, Tempest, Du Maurier, Cooper, Buchanan, Maugham, Lonsdale, Smith and Travers. But her public usually made vagueness a point of honour. When discussing the entertainment she provided, they would seldom condescend to be explicit. 'Had a good time the other evening with that fellow who slaps his pockets at that theatre next to the Carlton,' they would tell each other in the club or at the hairdresser. Miss Parker seldom gave them a bum steer; she knew very well when, if ever, they were in the mood for Chekhov or Galsworthy. She was a magnificent saleswoman. Customers seldom rang her up or came away from her establishment without sheaves of tickets.

Whenever I loitered near the counter she would include me among her recommendations. 'You'll want to see Mr Morley,' she'd tell them, and they seldom demurred. Strangely enough, another Miss Parker now presides over Hatchard's and though I sometimes hover there too, only very occasionally does she proffer one of my books in addition to the ones already selected. Still, it's sometimes worth a try and anyway I like Hatchard's almost as much as I used to like Ashton's.

Where the critics were concerned, Agate and Tynan and to a lesser extent St. John Ervine and Morgan counted with my fellow actors. A good notice from Trewin or Darlington cheered but it was Agate above all who made our hearts glow and our hands reach for the paste brush to enshrine his judgement in our press-cutting books. Agate was witty at his own expense, Tynan at ours. In the war Agate was often to be met at Heppel's in the Strand or Perkins in Piccadilly; both sold patent restoratives and soap for which there always seemed an endless supply of coupons. He once thrust unexpectedly into my hand a florin bearing the head of the Prince Regent, a part I once essayed. I was immensely proud and still occasionally turn out a drawer in a hopeless and unavailing quest for it. Like the medal once given me by the Pope (though not, I hasten to add, for any outstanding act of piety, but merely that he was giving them out to callers during Holy Year) it has vanished without trace but the memory of Agate lingers imperishably for me as for all my contemporaries. A schoolmaster who placed his pupils in their order of achievement. I was not among the top of the class, but my name wasn't quite at the bottom either.

At least it was not he who wrote, 'Mr Morley was trying in both senses of the word.' I was a member of a repertory theatre in Bournemouth in those days and I have never forgiven nor forgotten.

Fifty years is a short time in the theatre.

An actor must learn to live with criticism and not only the ones in his scrapbooks. The comments of his nearest and dearest often rankle insanely over the years. Gladys Cooper never forgot her mother's observation on the first night of her earliest triumph. 'You looked, dear, a trifle peaky.' There was Mrs Irving's celebrated aside to her husband as they drove home after his resounding triumph in *The Bells*: 'How much longer, Henry, are you going on making a fool of yourself?' Irving, to his everlasting credit, stopped the cab and put his wife out of it, never to speak to the lady again. 'What did you think of it then?' I asked my mother after she had watched me portray Shylock at the Royal Academy of Dramatic Art in my student days. 'I thought your fingernails were rather dirty, dear.'

Once, heavily disguised, I bestrode the stage as Oedipus and afterwards closely questioned a favourite aunt as to her reaction. 'Your mask,' she told me, 'looked exactly as if it was made of Sorbo sponge.'

'That is because it is made of Sorbo,' I told her roughly, and never again provided her with a complimentary seat.

On the first night of the first play I ever wrote I was handed a telegram as I left the stage door informing me that a Mr Wintle was safely home again after watching only the first act of what he trusted was the worst play he would ever be compelled to witness. 'I hope,' I told myself, 'it's not always going to be like this,' and of course it wasn't. In all the years since then no one else has ever bothered to telegraph, and the danger has now passed. For one thing the cost these days is prohibitive, and for another the post office closes a great deal earlier.

My Agents

Gordon Harbord, Nora Nelson King, Vincent Erne, Barry O'Brien, Miriam Warner, all had offices within walking distance of Leicester Square. Most of us visited them at least once a week, sometimes twice when we were resting. Through them we found employment at salaries ranging from four to fifteen pounds a week. Once arrived in their office we were told, 'Nothing today,' or were directed to even dingier offices where the managers were waiting to judge our suitability for the parts they were hoping to cast. If the salaries were small, the engagements were usually for forty weeks on the road with the third company of *The Private Secretary* which (so as not to hurt our feelings unduly) was referred to by them as the Blue or Red Company.

Nearly every West End success went on tour in the provinces, though seldom with the original cast. Nor did we expect to act in London during our apprenticeship. At some stage in his career the actor would decide, usually for himself, that he was West End material, put away his book of cherished theatrical lodgings and sit it out as long as the money lasted. Sometimes he had to return to the provinces for another ten years, sometimes for ever, in which case he hoped one day to become a provincial star of which there were perhaps fifty or so who commanded three-figure salaries.

There were also a large number of repertory companies, some of which changed the bill twice weekly and almost all of which (save in a few university towns or the big cities such as Liverpool) played twice nightly. In those days we got in a good deal of acting and told ourselves and our parents, if they were interested or remotely encouraging, that we were learning the business.

We got in a good deal of exercise, too, in search of it. We climbed innumerable flights of stairs, like postmen or parlourmaids, occasionally to be rewarded with a postcard entitling us to climb other staircases at the top of which we would wait patiently to be interviewed by our prospective employer. References were sometimes required in the form of press cuttings from *The Stage* or *The Wirral Advertiser*. Sometimes we even advertised in the former. 'Responsible gentleman, own wardrobe, play as cast, vacant Feb. 7, 14, 21st,' and so on with exceptions. Or 'Smartest Little Juvenile in the business, dresses well on and off, thanks previous management for offer and gift of handkerchiefs but must have terms.' But mostly the jobs came through the agents and in my case it was not until I had written my first play that I achieved someone I was proud to call my exclusive representative.

Once having acquired an agent of his very own, an actor parts with him or her at his peril. The ensuing proceedings are often more painful and costly than if he were to dissolve his marriage. He can usually survive a number of marriages but divorce from an agent puts him in the position of a racehorse owner who has changed stables too often. Such a man seldom wins races. An agent who has been 'jocked off', as the saying goes, is loath to see his ex-client in the frame. He likes to have the last word about him at the memorial service, but if not there, then at least on the telephone to managers still thinking of engaging him.

'I believe he may really have stopped drinking, at least for the present; it's certainly worth a try if you are not opening in London too soon.'

Or, 'No, I don't know who represents him these days, but I have an idea he prefers to spend most of his time in Fiji.'

Or, 'I certainly take my hat off to you, Alan, casting him in that part. I only hope he will remember to keep his teeth in. They say his last picture should have been retitled *The Battle of the Lower Plate*.'

As his client climbs the greasy pole of fame and fortune, the agent must be ready with the helping shove, and when, as must inevitably occur, he begins to slide down it, must ensure the progress is neither too painful nor too rapid. But his most important role is to convince others that the actor is in truth the likeable, dedicated artiste whom he imagines himself to be and not (as is often suspected) as mean as hell, as vain as a peacock, as witless as a dove and as treacherous as a snake. It is the agent who must open the wicker basket and encourage his pet to sway to the music which he has previously composed for him – a million dollars with a percentage of the gross receipts, first class travel, gargantuan expenses, star billing and a clause that live rabbits in the shape of hairdressers, make-up personnel and domestic staff must be constantly available, along with a concubine rabbit if required, though this is seldom written into the contract itself. In between dances he must be available day and night to satisfy the ceaseless demands of his charge. His is the hand that feeds and more often than not gets bitten.

Mind you, I am not speaking personally. I am always the most reasonable of men, one of the most likeable alive in point of fact. I never argue or complain, despise the script, insult the director, announce that if the money hasn't been paid I shall not be turning up for work on the morrow, or beef because my caravan on the lot is inferior to that of another artiste. My agent will confirm all this. Nor do I demand that when she has negotiated my contract she must necessarily watch me fulfilling it. A less reasonable fellow than I recently greeted his agent with: 'What about me on the box last night, then?'

'Splendid, boysie, much better than you led me to believe it was going to be. You were great, simply great.'

'The gap didn't bother you then?' persisted his client.

Realizing that there must have been a breakdown during transmission of which he was unaware, since he hadn't watched any part of it, his agent went for game and match. 'I'll tell you a funny thing, the breakdown seemed to help. It built suspense. Funny!'

'Very,' came back the riposte, 'since the whole programme was cancelled along, incidentally, with our contract.'

You can't win them all, though the celebrated American agent Abe Gresshler once tried very hard to do so. An inveterate poacher of talent, he was once persuaded that Clark Gable himself was waiting at the other end of a telephone to be represented by him. Seizing the instrument, he lost no time in arranging the contract, only to be called back a few minutes later by his prospective client.

'There's just one thing I forgot to ask you, Mr Gresshler; are you Jewish?' There was only the briefest of pauses while Mr Gresshler considered his reply, which was to become legendary.

'Not necessarily, Mr Gable.'

When I first met Mr Gresshler a few years ago he patted my cheek fondly and observed, 'Baby, I don't know what they are paying you but you're worth more!' And my first agent, Hayes Hunter, exuded the same air of confident salesmanship. He made my first contract with MGM, bluffing them into paying me several hundred pounds a week by informing them that I was independently wealthy and only worked for my own amusement. This got over the awkward fact that the only two previous engagements I had secured in the industry were at the rate of ten pounds a day and I had been sacked from both.

Some time after Hayes's death in the Blitz, I was lucky enough to become the client of Robin Fox, an old Harrovian who had been a solicitor before the war in which he won the Military Cross, and who combined the lethal charm of a prince of the Borgias with membership of the MCC. A consummate actor he was: when dealing with the Italian Film Industry, a father of the Mafia; when arranging the affairs of the Royal Court Theatre for his great friend George Devine, a potentate of the Treasury; when gambling with me on the Riviera, a member of the Greek syndicate.

At home in Cuckfield he was the squire, in management Diaghilev, and for the rest of the time by far and away the most amusing friend I ever made. When he died tragically of cancer, his partner and I soldiered on, trying, and often succeeding, to remember his precepts. He fitted his clients with ten-league boots and encouraged them to keep walking tall.

In these days few actors ever admit to earning a salary, only to accepting a challenge. It is up to his squire to see that the management pays for his knight's lance and shining armour and that he earns a substantial sum for the joust. No sensible Don Quixote grudges him his share of the purse, or is foolish enough to sight the next windmill until he is sure that Sancho Panza is once more at his side.

My Directors

Perhaps because I never cared for schoolmasters, I have never (save for one extraordinary exception) had much faith in directors. The exception was Tyrone Guthrie, who had a unique prescience where the theatre was concerned. His descent on the stage can be likened to Darwin's first visit to the Galapagos Islands. He closely examined the iguanas basking in the limelight, drew the necessary conclusions, propounded his theories in a series of dazzling experiments, and at what now seems to me a comparatively early age had worked himself to death. We are not likely to see his like again for a few centuries and meanwhile, you may ask, what and whom did he leave behind?

The sad answer is very little and no one. True, some of the theatres he founded are still ticking, but most of the actors he taught have already keeled over. As far as I know, he never bothered to teach any directors. Like Darwin, he was not believed in his lifetime, yet to know him was like meeting Moses coming down from Ararat.

You may argue that it was Noah who came down, or rather floated off that particular mountain, and you could be right, but I trust by now you will have grasped how I felt about him. There are a few men I have met who seemed to talk with God. Shaw was another.

'The sort of director I like,' Wilfrid Hyde White once confided, 'is one who will cheerfully fetch my script when I have left it in the motor.'

They are not all like that. I once indicated to Peter Brook that I could do with a Coca-Cola. I didn't really expect him to go himself, but hoped he would depute one of his assistants to do the necessary merchandising. In the end I was the one who went. When I returned he looked sadly at his watch.

'I thought,' I told him, 'that if I was going for the Coca-Cola I might as well have an early luncheon.' We didn't get on all that well; in point of fact, we didn't get on at all. Naturally the play was a great success; there is nothing like sustained strife backstage to ensure eventual triumph at the box office. The more harmony reigns, the less chance of what Peter might refer to (as he lives mostly abroad) as a *succès fou*.

A director's life is seldom a happy one. Merciful providence ordains that it is also usually comparatively brief. Actors survive a great deal longer. The theatre expels directors as men discard torch batteries. Once they fail to light a couple of times, no one bothers to recharge them. It is a trade that attracts the bully and the scholar in about equal proportions. A man steeped in the university tradition seldom wants to do anything but teach others what he never really managed to do himself. On the whole I find them easier to work with when they have had even less education than I had, but these are rare birds indeed.

Basil Dean (perhaps it may be safer to discuss directors who have exited off stage) was a fair example of the stern boss who brought to the theatre all the excitement of the executive washroom. He sat in the stalls separated from his worker puppets by the invisible curtain of executive privilege. He was not particularly good at understanding the workers, but now and again his brisk assembly lines produced a model which sold. He could be extremely unpleasant and often was. Once during the war I fought under his banner when he was in charge of providing entertainment for the troops. I rang up E.N.S.A. and by some mischance at his H.Q. got through to him personally and demanded a stage carpet to deaden the sound of my wheelchair in the drill halls; I was immersed in *The Man Who Came to Dinner* at the time.

'I think, Morley,' he told me, 'you are entitled to a carpet; you are playing the principal camps. Apply for allotment.' He took the war and the theatre seriously. On the whole life is easier when they don't.

One of the phenomena of the trade is how many of them are called Peter. There is no chosen name which so vividly expresses parental aspiration. Peter Ashmore was for some years my favourite; we shared success and the table wine over the midday meal. 'Lunch, boss?' he would enquire when the watch hands stood at attention. Over the Chianti we often used to get good ideas, not necessarily about the play. However, his greatest triumph as far as I was concerned was at breakfast one morning when he joined me at the Ritz and over the buttered eggs we were able to construct a scene which persuaded Peggy Ashcroft, my leading lady, that hers might be quite a good part after all and cajole her into remaining in the show.

Ashmore, alas, doesn't direct plays any more. He inherited a thriving mortuary business, disposed of it, and lives happily in Ireland. A director I haven't actually ever worked with always rates higher in my book and I in theirs, or so I like to believe. We tend to regard each other as uncut stones; modesty forbids I should use the word diamonds. Blakemore, I tell myself, or Pinter or Peter (another of them) Hall, I should like to give them a whirl sometime. I don't say they fall over themselves to reciprocate, but they sometimes purpurt to be willing to try.

I began, as all actors did between the wars, with the prompt copy of a play already running in the West End or else a copy of French's acting edition. Both had the moves written down, and we followed these without questioning the motive for them. We understood that if X says his line while crossing to fireplace Down Left, he will not be standing in front of Y whose turn it is to speak next. In essence this is the reason actors cross and recross a stage. Nowadays actors tend to argue over such matters and the director has to rack his brains to provide motivation to avoid a pile-up.

'You move,' he tells him, 'because you are considering blowing out your brains and there is a gun in the writing desk, top drawer left.' The actor crosses, fails to open the drawer because it is a dummy and expostulates.

'Halfway across,' concedes the director, 'you decide not to blow them out.'

'Then,' replies the actor, 'why don't I stay Centre?'

'You can pause briefly,' concedes his director, 'but I want you to have second thoughts and be clear of Miss Y when she speaks.'

'It's a bit difficult,' the actor will argue, 'to get that over unless there is a real gun and a real drawer.'

'You shall have one at the dress rehearsal,' he is promised, but the promise is never kept and by that time he has got used to the move like any other circus pony.

We are living in a time when directors have become the favourite pupils of the critics. Writing their reports, they extol the avant-garde ragamuffin who sets his *Hamlet* in a submarine or can, with the extreme economy of the single spotlight, suggest the hopelessness of a public urinal.

'Cystitis,' the critic will tell us, 'does not immediately suggest a rewarding subject for a critic's evening, but I came away from *Bladders and Blood* with an extraordinary sense of elation. The theatre lives again!'

You may think part of the blame belongs to the playwright who, from a hospital bed, originally conceived the idea, but it is the director more than the actor or the manager or the playwright who so often encourages the playgoer to keep his distance and wait happily for a revival of *The King and I*. Directors are dead keen. Their work span is limited to six weeks' rehearsals at a time, after which even the most dedicated loses interest and opts not to revisit his stomping ground; indeed, is often prevented from doing so in the case of *Bladders and Blood* which has closed.

Like the picked troops of the SAS regiment they must be off on another assault course, one which they may even be allowed to devise. Teaching unwilling recruits to cope with precipitously raked stages, narrow staircases from which banisters have been removed, leading to perilous rostrums. 'How else,' they will tell the actors tottering in terror, blinded by spotlights and clothed in strait-jackets, 'can we suggest Mortlake Brewery? For heaven's sake get on with it, old man, and don't make difficulties.'

Theatre directors must earn a living like everyone else, and in order to ensure some continuity of employment they constantly attract attention to themselves. Life for them is easier when they choose to direct a classic or a musical. With the latter the audience will search their programmes to discover who got it all together and a man like Harold Prince often emerges as the real star of the evening, but with Shakespeare it is not enough for the director merely to cast the play and let the actors learn and speak the text, as was demonstrated in the recent hopeless effort of the British Broadcasting Corporation to record the Bard more or less straight.

During my schooldays I was subjected to periodical visits from Sir Ben Greet and his company of players, who performed in the quadrangle of Wellington College in much the same style. Later I was to invade large private schools for special matinées with Sir Frank Benson's Troupe. For some reason the bus seldom managed to drive into the grounds, and wearing doublets and laddered hose or embroidered gowns we would scuttle the last hundred yards, watched by our apprehensive victims from the classroom windows.

In extenuation I can only plead that we were not paid extra for special matinées, that we were expected to perform six and sometimes eight different Shakespearian plays every week, and that some of us drank rather heavily. It was a therapeutic experience for the scholars and myself. Ever since, I have avoided acting Shakespeare and the demon alcohol, at least until the curtain is down.

If my approach to directors has on the whole been a little short of idolatry, it is not to say that I haven't at times benefited from their constant efforts to encourage me to speak the text and position me as often as they could with my back to the audience to cure an obsessional desire to gaze out front in order to reassure myself that you are still enjoying yourselves, and indeed that you have come at all.

My Scripts

I read with a pang of displeasure, in the house magazine of the Windsor Repertory Company, that plans were afoot in Grimsby or some other seaport to revive *The White Sheep Of The Family*, a play by Ian Hay which I once threw into the Indian Ocean.

Emboldened by alcohol, I was explaining to a fellow passenger the criteria by which I was accustomed to judge a script and having just received a copy of this one, I removed it from the envelope and pretended to examine it for conformity by weighing it in my hand. Turning it upside down in order to ascertain the length of the speeches without troubling to read them, I promptly discarded it into the briny. A grave error; it ran and ran but without my participation in the profits.

Like most actors I get sent a certain number of scripts by the authors themselves, and what most of us look for on these occasions is cleanliness. I don't, of course, mean in the text itself, but if there are signs of wear and tear, particularly with the cover, you can be pretty sure you are not holding an instantly recognizable masterpiece in your hand.

There have been instances of plays such as *Journey's End* being submitted to a score of managements and leading men before becoming world beaters, but these are the exceptions. My own reaction is to examine the manuscript carefully for traces of Ralph Richardson's thumb-prints. Once satisfied as to the mint condition of the folio, one is still aware of how slim the chance of a strike. Good plays, like welcome guests, seldom arrive unexpectedly although my own first effort was accepted, when it arrived unbidden through the mail box, by Marie Tempest forty years ago. It wasn't, as it turned out, a very wise decision on her part, but I was never in any doubt why she had made it. She hadn't another play she wanted to do, she thought it could be improved and I had had the play beautifully typed by Ethel Christian and wisely sent her the top copy. Ethel used a special kind of typewriter ribbon of vivid blue and her name on the title page reassured. When you collected the scripts she was always encouraging. This one, she would tell you, is a smasher, my girls were simply overboard about it. We went on our way consoled by the reflection that we had given such pleasure to the staff. Like hop pickers, we told ourselves, they enjoyed their work.

Plays arriving on my desk by post are usually accompanied by a stamped and addressed envelope in which to return them. There is also a note from the author indicating the role for which he has one in mind, and sometimes the vague promise that it could be enlarged at some future date, were I to undertake it. These go straight into the accompanying envelope and after a decent interval of lying in wait on the table, go winging back to the sender. It is always a mistake to build up one's own part at the expense of others in the cast, indeed as one grows older and bolder one seeks to shed as many lines as possible. My distinguished mother-in-law seldom bothered to learn all the lines allotted to her. At the dress rehearsal any lingering hopes held by the author or the director that Gladys might have committed them to memory and be keeping them in reserve vanished. By then, too, she hadn't left a lot of time for argument.

Another great performer – adept at cutting out the sage-brush – Beatrice Lillie, was apparently so unfamiliar with the text the night before we were due to open a play of mine at Oxford that the management engaged a stand-by who (already seated in the auditorium) was to proceed on stage should a red light flash in the orchestra pit and Miss Lillie forget not only the lines but the time of the opening performance. The light flashed green, just in time for the twelfth man to catch the last train to London. Miss Lillie's performance that evening was that of a master at the bridge table; after one or two daring finesses she laid down her hand and boldly claimed the rest of the tricks without bothering to play them.

It is the aim of every actor to persuade his public that he has made the hand work no matter what cards have been dealt him by the playwright. It was Miss Tempest who taught me that it is always advisable not to encourage the latter to think he has dealt one a small slam.

At the first reading of a play she would pause in feigned

astonishment at her cue line and peer at the author in silence until the stage manager had the courage to point out that it was now her turn to speak. 'I am just wondering,' she would then remark, 'whether I really have to say this line, Mr...'

She made a point of never remembering the playwright's name.

'Why ever not?' he would ask meekly.

'It's just that I've said it so often before in all my other plays.' She would flash a smile and then surprisingly proceed to say it, although with no great conviction. Miss Tempest when reading aloud on these occasions took care to spread a trail of false emphasis and alarm and despondency in the hearts of her supporting cast. The magic came later.

Borrowing from Miss Tempest, I once nearly flummoxed the great Peter Ustinov himself by my first reading of *Half Way Up A Tree* which I felt I had left well up in the branches when the time came for luncheon at Scott's. 'You know, Mr Morley,' the manager's wife told me, 'there can be no question of any interpolations. We have script approval.'

'I only wish I had,' I told her and relapsed into moody silence. Ustinov's thoughts were elsewhere; he was planning simultaneous productions of his play in New York, Paris and Berlin. As it happened, he was the one with the interpolations; he kept thinking of additional dialogue and sending it to us air mail while he sweated it out in Boston or Newhaven.

I am not, of course, referring to the Sussex town where one takes off for Dieppe but the one in Connecticut where one hopefully embarks for Broadway. As there was always some doubt as to who was to speak the new lines, and when exactly, I used to offer them round fairly indiscriminately. There are always takers for new lines by other actors; myself, I can only learn a few at a time. In the end Peter seemed quite happy and so did I, the play contrary to my early forebodings running for a couple of years. When I left the cast, the play sailed merrily on with Jimmy Edwards, a great one for improving texts on the spur of the moment. Seizing a biscuit one evening he proceeded to munch, and noticed a hint of disapproval in the eyes of his leading lady. 'I hope,' he told her, 'you do not object to my masticating in the drawing room?' His co-star slammed down her tea cup and left the stage. 'I do not intend to sit and listen to filth,' she told the stage manager, 'Equity contract or no Equity contract.'

The other day there arrived in the post a play by an old friend whose works up to now have passed me by. In accepting it I realise it may indeed mark the end of our friendship. Dramatists, when I do act their plays, are not always satisfied by my reading of their lines. 'It's not quite what I wrote, old man,' they will urge from the stalls during rehearsals. 'It's the gist,' I tell them, 'just listen again carefully.'

Summing Up

Timing is all. The actor and the jockey must decide the pace at which the race is to be run. An actor cannot succeed until he has learnt to wait, but not to wait too long, for the laughs. A good actor even dies on the day the obituary columns are not too crowded. My supreme good fortune was to have timed my own entry into the acting game. Much more is demanded of the players today than a desire to be noticed and have a good time. Good times are scarce. So often nowadays the theatre becomes the operating theatre. The actor submits to the director's knife, a dedicated patient in the pursuit of knowledge rather than happiness.

Some of my agile contemporaries still manage to climb on to the table and even to enjoy themselves, clothed in hessian, submitting to modern brain surgery techniques, or (to change the metaphor) manage to secure for themselves a fleeting foothold on the caravan as it trundles into the future. I am the dog that barks, content to be left behind enjoying the last rays of the sinking sun. Not, I trust, a melancholy dog, knowing I was extremely fortunate to have had my day and that it came when it did.

Increasingly the audience is not there on the night but will come later, when the series or the film is screened. The actor learns to do without them and (even when he returns to the theatre) to minimize their effect on his performance. For me it is the House, which even if it is only half-full may make the evening a delight and make it possible to play the role over and over again, because no two evenings in the theatre are ever the same.

I try not to perfect my own performance but that of the audience. It is a game of patience played with a missing card, a jigsaw to be completed with one of the pieces lost, which has enthralled and delighted me for more than fifty years.

Once in a while you catch the big wave, but always you must turn the board around and paddle out to sea again. Not that I ever managed to stay on a surf-board for more than a few seconds. Once, carrying the dead wood out of the surf in Hawaii, I found one of the children in tears. 'They are laughing at you, Father,' she said.

'So they should,' I comforted. 'That's what I'm here for.'

But, like the great George Robey, I may occasionally abjure them to restrain their hilarity with a modicum of reserve. It never does to make too big a fool of oneself – which is why, I suppose, I go to the theatre so seldom these days with the enforced companionship of my hearing aid. It is no good pretending it makes an ideal partner. I find it impossible to forecast the creature's mood. Coaxed into listening attentively for part of the performance, it will often grow impatient and start to emit a shrill whistle. We are both inordinately fond of Mr John Wood, especially when he is in a piece by Mr Stoppard, which seems to us to be a combination of the cleverest actor and playwright alive. We would go anywhere to see a play by Simon Gray and almost anywhere for one by Alan Ayckbourn.

Pinter worries. The long pauses make me afraid that one of us has packed up. Our best evening for a long time was spent hearing *Flowers for Algernon*. I switched off and went backstage to assure Mr Crawford it would run for ever. It lasted a month. I am not a good judge these days if, indeed, ever I was. In management for a year or two my partners and I put on some fourteen plays and won about four of the tricks. My contribution was to insist on sofas and armchairs and cutting out the desk work and indeed the desk itself. I doubt if it helped much.

Nevertheless we enjoyed ourselves hugely, sometimes even at our own expense. One of the plays we presented dealt with papal countesses and unfrocked priests. It lost a small fortune. 'I am surprised at your putting on a play such as this, Morley,' an elderly backstage visitor remarked.

Religion is a subject which invariably leads to unpleasantness. Unpleasantness was something the theatregoer only took to comparatively recently; before then there were definite taboos. The Lord Chamberlain supplied a list of them on demand. In some ways it made life easier; certainly the theatre didn't lose half as much money as it does now. Along with the french windows and the chintz armchairs went the carpet under which certain matters such as incest, homosexuality, blasphemy were firmly swept. We lost a lot of playgoers when we took up the carpet.

AUSTRALASIA
REVISITED

Kiwi Polish

Saturdays are by tradition quiet days in New Zealand. In Auckland everything closes down by noon on Fridays to enable the inhabitants to get clear of the place in good time. Visitors from Singapore and even Fiji search in vain for the slightest sign of jollification. Here are no massage parlours, no public squares filled with the gay transvestite crowd.

A race meeting was to be soberly conducted in the country on Saturday, with the Jockey Club taking displayed advertisements in the local press to announce that for one meeting only members need not wear ties in the enclosure because of a predicted heat wave which, alas, never materialized.

Elsewhere shorts are worn by men and boys, lending weight to the Baden-Powell theory that a gentle breeze around the genitals is the surest guarantee of pure thought and deed.

New Zealanders wish fervently that other lands were as well ordered as their own, the papers give little hint that such indeed is not the case, reserving their front pages for discussions on forthcoming bowling matches. 'Heads will Roll on the Greens' is the sanguine and sanguinary prediction. Tucked away discreetly is a reference to the current problem of New Zealand slaughtermen and the insistence of a government inspector from Iran that lambs must now be slaughtered when fully conscious and facing towards Mecca.

Few New Zealanders have been to Mecca, and an air of despondency persists here as indeed in the Common Market itself. The days when butter was loaded continuously at the docks are gone, along with the steamers. The machinery still lies rusting on the quays but new markets for butter are hard to find. Has anyone thought of Tibet, where they drink it apparently in tea?

Despondency exists but not alarm, though grandparents are occasionally perplexed by the latitude now granted to their progeny. My daughter, one of them told me, actually asks her daughter what she would like for breakfast. Naturally by the time she's cooked it the child has changed her mind.

Children are not encouraged to change their minds, or weren't until quite recently. They got into sailing and cricket and rugby and stayed in them for their lives. Not the girls, of course, they had the children and later on bowling. Recently there has been a feeling that they too should be permitted to sail. A club has been formed to instruct them in the art, and wives now commandeer their husbands' yachts during the week and bash them against the jetties. But what are boats for except to keep trim, and no New Zealand husband can forbear to point out to the little woman that but for her carelessness they would be at sea by this time instead of still tied up while the hull is being repainted. At sea, perhaps, is an over-statement; here, as in Sydney, boats seldom leave harbour. Auckland's harbour is larger even than Sydney's.

We ventured forth on Sunday ourselves, slightly ashamed that our craft should have Taxi Cat so boldly displayed on the side.

On a remote island, once famous as a prison camp in World War I, we were entertained by a Dutchman with stories of his prowess as a cook but given meat pies warmed through cellophane while wife and grandchildren sailed away on a catamaran to the pictures. Almost as disappointing an experience as the fishing. We watched cormorants swooping, and swooped in our turn and caught nothing. In all that vast harbour there were no fish willing to be hauled aboard. It's becoming a scandal, our waterboatman told us, people are beginning to complain.

'To whom?' I asked.

'That's the trouble,' he replied. 'The Japanese, I suppose, as usual.'

'Not that it does any good. We have the same trouble at British Leyland,' I comforted him.

The happiest man I met grows wine, an ex-gum digger from Macedonia, whose citizens before the war had something of a monopoly of gum-digging hereabouts. It was a calling requiring a stout heart and, of course, gum boots. They sought the substance like truffle hounds, a kind of adolescent amber which fetched good prices. But with the coming of synthetic resin, Macedonians took to growing wine. Our host's three sons who respectively tended the grapes, made the wine and sold the stuff, told me that. You need three of them in this business, though father had apparently started on his own and for some reason married his wife in Yugoslavia by proxy.

We drank the wine of the house, which doesn't come on the market, and our hostess fell backwards into the pool while taking our picture, as gracefully as Katharine Hepburn herself.

'My wife always tends to overdo things,' remarked her husband. 'She wanted to go on and have daughters but I told her enough is enough. It's not as if we were sheep farmers.' Slightly bemused, we left just in time to catch the Sydney plane.

New Zealand, I am happy to report, is alive and well and living at the other end of the Pacific Ocean.

Dateline Melbourne

Dining last night in Sydney with Mr Ellis Irving, an actor whom I have known for many years and whose word I can accept without question, I learnt to my amazement that the projected invasion (which I reported on a short while ago) apparently was cancelled at the last moment. No Russian troops landed in Sydney or anywhere else in Australia and whatever dispatches may have been received in Tudor Street, I am able categorically to deny. My reliable source and I had a most pleasant evening over mud crabs and a bottle of Reisling, the wine going down almost equally as well as the crabs, which by the end of the meal were deposited for a considerable distance around us, bibs and finger bowls notwithstanding. As is often the way with crustaceans, the meat is sweeter on the other side of the claw. The problem is how to crack the spidery shells and not grow too exhausted to continue feasting.

How pleasant afterwards to deal with a pêche melba and what a relief. There seemed little point in hanging on in Sydney, so I moved to Melbourne. The last few days in the New South Wales area have been extremely wet and windy. Hurricane weather, as the natives call it, but although the television has featured extensive floods and the inevitable movement of the elderly back to the schoolrooms and requisitioned drill halls, I really saw no point in adding, by close questioning, to the troubles of those whose homes had been carried away. The authorities here advise seeking refuge in an emergency in the smallest room of the house but then which of us doesn't have to do so from time to time.

As earlier explorers have pointed out, Melbourne, the capital of Victoria (how these place names help in understanding the ambience and period of all these cities), is situated on the banks of the Yarra

River. It is in fact no more than a leisurely flowing ditch and there is a popular theory that not only does it flow backwards but also upside-down; thus clear water is only to be found *under* the rather muddy surface. On its banks this morning I launched the annual raft regatta appeal in the company of two employees of a popular local soda pop factory dressed as Vikings and a raft made entirely of the empty tins in which the mixture is normally contained.

Several local television networks covered the ceremony and it must have seemed to them a welcome break from the happenings they normally record. For, in truth, this staid, rather placid backwater is also something of a permanent disaster area. In summer some part of the surrounding bush country is nearly always alight and the owners of charred properties are interviewed, against a background of acrid smoke by the side of gutted motor cars and burnt-down bungalows, commenting on the fact that they just managed to save the mother-in-law but not, alas, the budgies.

In the spring they are baling out parlours or wading along newly opened canals, pushing improvised barges made out of packing-cases containing all their worldly goods with the possible exception of the piano, which floated off independently at the height of the holocaust. In the autumn they are pictured standing on the roof which once sheltered their loved ones but now has been deposited by a hurricane a good deal further than they are able to carry it back.

What is so remarkable about the demeanour of those who will, hopefully, appear only once in their lives in front of the lenses of eager newshounds, is their quite extraordinary cheerfulness. Either all properties around here are grossly over-insured or the pioneer spirit still persists among the citizens and the knowledge that what didn't take much to knock down won't take all that long to knock up once more.

When disaster strikes the stiff upper lip is much in evidence. The fact that it is also firmly clamped to the lower one makes it sometimes difficult to understand what it was that actually hit them. Then, too, almost all Australian motor cars are natural killers; almost twice as many people die in road accidents in this country than anywhere else in the world – always allowing for statistical adjustment – but the motor car out here has another even more lethal prerequisite, a long tradition of instant combustion. Parked amidst others on race tracks, beaches or picnic areas, they unaccountably burst into flames and thus start a chain of bonfires among other vehicles, causing the occupants, snoozing after a heavy meal or resting from the labours of love, to run for their lives. Australians are notoriously carefree when it comes to the disposal of litter or cigarette ends but it is generally accepted that motor cars often get so depressed at careless handling and too much exercise that, driven to desperation, they commit *hari-kiri*.

Melbourne is, of course, almost continuously strike-bound; one day it is the trams, the next the trains, on the third day both are struck, along with the fire brigades and the dustmen. Thus most Australians need their cars on weekdays to get to and from their work and to transport their garbage to a convenient tip, of which there is no shortage in these parts, but at weekends they simply get in them and go for a drive.

The sad thing is that with all the traffic on the roads and quite often in the nearby ditches, you never see an English model. Always a do-it-yourself nation, they like to be personally responsible for any breakdown which may occur. The Prime Minister, when he is not being unceremoniously butted by one of his own bulls actively campaigned to move the Olympics from Moscow to this city and one could not help wishing him success. Athletes have it far too good with all these carefully raked running tracks and deep sanded pits. It might do them good to hold their childish encounters in genuine bush country, vaulting kangaroo fences and pounding dried river beds, throwing their hammers into impenetrable scrub land, running marathons in the local hills. This is presumably what the Greeks did when they first set out and the Australian Government would, as always, dearly like to put back the clock, if it unfortunately hadn't already stopped, in the land where Lord Melbourne still rules.

I was all packed to visit Adelaide when chancing to turn on the television I was horrified to discover they were suffering from a plague of mice. Hundreds of thousands of the small creatures, devouring everything in their path. I did not come all the way out here to be snapped up along with the cheese and the grain, so thought it prudent to visit Canberra instead. Canberra is the headquarters of a peacekeeping force fulfilling much the same function as Brasilia. The politicians, diplomats and civil servants who serve their time in this extremely beautiful open prison are expected to impinge as little as possible on the lives of the ordinary citizens and although escape from Canberra itself is comparatively simple, most of the inmates resign themselves cheerfully to the enforced inactivity which the regime demands.

Built around an artificial lake and dominated by an enormous war memorial, the architecture varies from the grandiose early Lutyens to the late Nissen Hut. The latter, built in the justified expectation of the growth of bureaucracy just after the war have, like our own prefabs, survived despite predictions that they would succumb in early childhood, and lived on to ripe old age.

The Houses of Parliament, like the present Prime Minister, are built of altogether sterner stuff. In the beautifully air-conditioned chamber, replete with mace and speaker in full-bottomed wig, Mr Fraser reclines in a swivel chair surveying his class like the headmaster of a good comprehensive school faced with the difficulties of a new term and some older boys who should have left long ago and continue to set a rather bad example to the newcomers.

Headmasters, alas, are seldom concerned with education. Administration is their game and Mr Fraser gives the impression that he personally could function a good deal more effectively if he was not for ever having to take time off to address the school. True, he delegates authority to his prefects, summoning them one at a time to sit beside him while he tells them what he expects them to say and how he wishes them to say it. They scurry off to the despatch box and, clothed with a little brief authority, do their best to impersonate their master's manner and voice, the latter, alas, to these battered old English ears often proving largely inaudible. While I was there the Head spoke at more than his usual length about the way the Russians were generally letting down the side.

During this rather lengthy pi jaw the boys opposite were at pains to try and persuade him that his words were wasted on them, some of the bolder spirits repeatedly leaving for the cloakrooms without first raising their hands to obtain the required permission. Others slept while a number spent the time folding circulars and positioning them in envelopes, although no one actually interrupted the flow to request a stamp.

If Mr Fraser does not suffer boys gladly he seems more tolerant than most of his calling to parents and possibly elder sisters. His own wife and daughter and a row of beaming ministerial wives followed his every word with the keenest enjoyment and rapt attention normally afforded to visiting dignitaries and the Master himself on school speech days. Unaccountably I dozed off, was tapped on the shoulder by a vigilant press secretary and conducted to the bar. We were invited for drinks later in the presidential suite but, alas, I had to decline as I had to return to Melbourne. I learnt, however, that Mr Fraser is surprisingly unpunctual; he catches aeroplanes at the last moment, confident that in any case they will wait for him and, like our own Mrs Thatcher, can be a trifle peremptory with those whom he feels are wasting his time of which, one gathers, there are a surprising number. Both, one feels, have the best interests of the school at heart.

Down Under and Out

On wet afternoons in Cheltenham when I was rather younger I would borrow a pudding basin from the cook, half fill it with water, place a Swan Vesta on the surface and inscribe a card announcing FLOATING MATCH. TO VIEW ONE PENNY. Reluctantly my parents would occasionally oblige with a coin but seldom my sister.

'We've had it, Bobby,' she used to tell me. I have had all my life a fatal tendency to stretch the joke.

I bethought me of Cheltenham when I finally reached the Bimini Wild Life Park after a desperate search among the Dandenongs, a range of hills beyond Melbourne where every other house is a restaurant bearing the message, mysterious to the uninitiated, 'BYO,'which means bring your own Fosters or whatever, or drink lemonade.

The Bimini Wild Life Park is signposted from all directions but we kept missing the turning which led into the Reserve itself until finally locating a rough cart track which ended abruptly in front of a small bungalow, the front sitting-room of which sported a soft drink dispenser and a more than ordinarily enraged cockatoo.

It is only fair that we reporters should sometimes go ahead of our readers to spy out the land; indeed it is our duty and privilege to do so in the case of civil strife and major catastrophe. The Bimini Wild Life Park must surely come under the latter heading.

Half a dozen sun-blackened fields are loosely divided from each other by sagging wires, presumably lest the chickens housed in one paddock should do battle with the hamsters segregated in another. There was a pond with frogs and a hutch with several rabbits. The centrepiece of this macabre collection was a display of abandoned motor car tyres and spare parts in which a kangaroo, a wallaby and a peacock foraged dejectedly. Some effort had been made here to recreate the natural habitat of the marsupials at least, but it was not enough, surely. I was tempted to demand the return of the gate money and then remembered the pudding basin.

'Live and let live' is my motto, which is one of the reasons why I thought it prudent to leave Melbourne before the duck shooting began in earnest. For some time the television and press have carried warnings of the impending danger. Australians are famous for getting their heads shot off during the mad month of March, or drowning in icy water while attempting to retrieve their retrievers similarly employed with a dead bird.

One of the more arcane programmes put out by government sources here recently is an educational film showing a would-be hunter in the act of 'Dialling a Duck'. The telephone appears to be growing in the bulrushes, and anyone can pick it up and enquire of the answering service in which direction the birds are currently flying. My local *Tasman Mercury* reports that at least two were killed (humans, not ducks) on the first day and another had his eye shot out by a friend whose own wasn't in as yet. As for the ducks, they take temporary refuge in the local parks and Botanical Gardens.

Ninety per cent of the tourists who come to Hobart go to Port Arthur as soon as they arrive. The other great attraction is the Casino, the only one in Australia to date, although plans are on foot to open another in Darwin which badly needs an aid to survival as a tourist trap after the disastrous earthquake, or was it a cyclone – how short is memory, alas.

The memory of the tragedy which overtook Hobart in '76 is still fresh, however. Almost exactly five years ago a tanker laden with zinc from the smelting works upstream rammed the bridge which is Hobart's lifeline with its two harbour shores and sank along with eight cars crossing at the time. Only a few bodies were ever recovered, and cars and ship lie on the river bed under the impenetrable silt. It took three years for the bridge to be rebuilt, along with the courage of the citizens who live on the further shore.

Port Arthur, however, is safely behind them and is now a National Park, preserving (as far as possible after demolition and two disastrous fires) its grim history of sado-masochism as it was practised for thirty years during the latter part of last century when the penal settlement there took root, blossomed and finally – and much to the annoyance of those who employed cheap labour thereabouts – expired.

It's a small world but somehow I didn't expect to find Tony Armstrong-Jones already *in situ* snapping the model prison, as the block devoted to solitary confinement used to be called. Prisoners were kept in silence and darkness, being forced to wear a visor over the face when visiting divine service and, when passing each other in the corridors, to proceed back to back. Nowadays visitors are treated to a film reproducing conditions under which the settlement operated and small children clap with glee when shown pictures, admittedly largely imaginary, of dogs who were kept chained and ravenous a few inches apart and housed in barrels to prevent escapes across the neck of the Peninsula on which the colony was sited.

There was also a train running from the nearest town and powered by convicts to convey VIPs on tours of inspection. The track ran up and down dale for a distance of eight miles and the only concession made to unfortunate handlers was permission to ride downhill if not too exhausted to climb aboard.

Juvenile offenders, who from the age of nine could be deported from Britain for stealing a pheasant, or even a book, were housed separately and taught a trade at which, when they had become proficient, they were expected to earn their living, and were indentured to an apprentice master and, curious to relate, often subsequently prospered and started businesses of their own throughout the colony.

The cheerful guide recounted fearful tales of bands of convicts who did escape, and how often the smallest ones were eaten by their companions and the survivors took to bush-ranging with considerable success. Quite how they avoided the dogs was never explained, but studying the pictures afterwards I decided a quick leap over the barrels would have been just feasible, supposing myself to be in better condition than I am today and that the guards who were supposed to be patrolling at the time were otherwise engaged. Swimming was out of the question – apparently the sharks in those days were as hungry as everyone else.

It started to rain and I sought shelter in the lunatic asylum, only recently shut down, apparently. But then I suppose by now there are too many of us at $2.00 a time. In the evening I sought solace at the roulette table in company with a fellow from the *Guardian* still keeping his readers in touch with the cricket scene, which seems to have mercifully faded.

Brisbane, or rather Surfers' Paradise, is not quite the sun-drenched playground I was expecting. The winds which lash the surf also bring heavy cloud banks and tropical downpours and the coastline is somewhat marred with skyscrapers in all stages of development and decorated with enormous banners indicating that whatever else awaits completion, the letting office is open for business.

Here, the special delicacies in the eateries are mud crab and Brisbane bugs, a delectable crayfish. There are miles and miles of sand, some intrepid surfers and, it must be confessed, a goodly number of bathing fatalities due to the dangerous and seemingly ever-present rip tides.

Across the lagoon from our condominium is the home of the late Gladys Moncrieff who reigned supreme on the Australian musical comedy stage for fifty years and appeared for five of them in *The Maid of the Mountains*. In those bygone days, plays seemed to manage to survive longer than the fortnight that is now a more usual period for a visiting company. What, you may ask, has happened to the theatre and what to Gladys? The latter question is more easily answered; she died and was buried and visitors passing her home on excursion boats still buy roses and gladioli and attempt to hurl them on to the lawn which comes down to the water edge, just as Gladys was wont to do if the boat was sufficiently full; and her friend and companion for many years, Elsie Wilson, continues to do to this very day.

There is loyalty for you and, catching a little of the mood, I myself opened the latest memorial to her, a bar hung with old photographs of the star and a restaurant in which every dish is named after one of her triumphs. We had Crab Salad Iolanthe, Veal Blue Mazurka, Mousse Chocolate Soldier and Coffee Merry Widow. Melba, who had to content herself with toast and ice-cream, once heard Miss Moncrieff at an audition when she was unwise enough to attempt one of the Div's own arias, and firmly advised her to stick to musical comedy.

Later, when they met again at a charity concert, she was reported to have reprimanded our Gladys for mispronunciation. The word, she told her is 'love, dear, with an O, not a U'. Melba, they say, was rather devoid of human affection, but Gladys Moncrieff was 'luv' to all who knew her and to a great many of those who did not.

To travel north is the dream of many Australians who find life in Sydney, Melbourne and even Brisbane passing too quickly in a dull round of surburban routine. They dream of the day when with the toilet training, the school run, the part-time job behind the counter of the fast food kiosk or the bar of the local finished, they can uproot sticks and their old man and move on to pastures new – a small banana plantation or a pineapple farm in the rain forest beyond Cairns. Luckily perhaps for most, it must remain a dream, but some are valiant enough to reach the Northern Tip of Queensland where the road ends abruptly; there they grow sugar cane, construct fish traps and scratch some sort of a living tending the occasional paw-paw. It is not a particularly easy life but then life is no longer as easy as it was in any part of this once happy-go-lucky country, where unions and government wrestle for power and they say Mr Fraser sleeps with a photograph of Mrs Thatcher under his pillow; or it could just possibly be the other way round.

The Starfish Encounter

I have had my leg for over a month now. Purists may argue that I have had it a good deal longer, over seventy years, but it now has a distinct identity enabling it to be counted outside the body corpulent to which it undoubtedly belongs in more peaceful times.

At breakfast I am inclined to issue bulletins as to its progress. The leg, I tell them, played up a bit towards dawn. The leg seems a mite less red after my bath. Occasionally I invite inspection from a near relative and every now and then my doctor. At this stage the latter is somewhat non-commital, he is awaiting a sheaf of medical notes from Australia bringing an up-to-date assessment of the problem, which, alas, I omitted to pack.

I took to bathing a good deal in Australia. Dunking oneself in the surf is a practice very common among geriatrics on Bondi and in my case Balmoral beaches. Elderly gentlemen of approximately twice my age paddle happily at the double along the sands. Emulating their example at a slow walk I stepped, apparently, on a dead starfish or similar decaying matter. A week later what I had mistaken for advanced sunburn manifested itself as cellulitis. My wife ringing up to cry off an engagement to lunch was comforted by an old friend, a lady who came out to the Antipodes as a girl, married a native and has adjusted remarkably well to a life in the colonies. 'He is lucky it's a matter of skin,' she remarked, 'they have the weirdest collection of infections out here – snakes, spiders and jelly-fish – and have learnt to cope remarkably well. They are splendid too at accidents, so many have their heads half lopped off sailing in the harbour when they forget to duck. If Robert had anything else the matter I would have advised waiting until he gets home.'

There was no question of waiting; by this time I was tucked up in one of Sydney's largest hospitals playing my part in the inevitable soap opera. How fortunate we are these days, patients and nursing staff alike. If anyone doesn't know his role by now he has simply omitted to buy a television set. Cast as the spoiled and by no means seriously ill eccentric, I spend happy hours questioning the efficient performance of the drip and the consistency of the omelettes, frequently demanding an adjustment of the former and the removal of the latter in favour of a plain poached egg. Once, but only once, I rang the emergency bell, when I needed immediate adjustment of my television screen. The room suddenly filled with menace. Interns came flying and had to be forcibly restrained from leaping on my chest to restore the heart beat. An oxygen cylinder was trundled into the room. Like a fireman responding to a call someone was hastily adjusting a mask. I managed to stop the rot only just in time. Releasing myself from the grip of a couple of nurses I made my needs known. 'It's the vertical hold,' I told them, 'I think it's at the back.' It was impossible not to have confidence in my consultant. Periodically he would uncover my leg in the company of an admiring coterie of students and matron and, having enquired how I thought I was feeling, address the supporting cast in a confidential tone. By straining my ears I would occasionally catch such phrases as, 'Gentlemen I propose to enlarge the spectrum.' 'In the event of any of these blisters actually bursting I shall require a culture.'

Considering that I am something of a vintage model I was disappointed that even the most junior staff sought fit to criticize the bodywork. There would, I felt, have been a good deal more admiration lavished on my condition if I had been an '08 Bugatti or Hispano. As it was, I grew tired of constant comments about my weight and slightly rusty suspension and forbade any further disparagement in my hearing.

'Polish up the gig lamps,' I told them. 'Don't look too hard beneath the bonnet and let's get out of here.' When I finally was once more adjudged fit for the road I was sent on my way with six different bottles of pills and the inevitable diet sheet counselling me to avoid almost all the food to which I have grown accustomed and substituting dishes too fearsome to contemplate. In my experience there is always an out on these occasions as they invariably include some substance of which one has never heard, thus invalidating the whole rigmarole.

The two lessons I have learnt are not to go barefoot and never, never after the age of seven or so act for relatives. My son Wilton, whose original idea it had been to present his aged parent in Sydney, spent an unhappy three weeks returning the customers' money, as I sat foot on cushion on the balcony of his apartment gazing out on Sydney harbour. It is the ambition of every Aussie to acquire property which commands a view of the Opera House and, when they have one, to save and borrow to get a second. My son is now, alas, back to square one but at least he managed to extricate us without forfeit from an unlikely engagement performing *The Old Country* in the ballroom of the Hilton Hotel in Singapore. The idea was the patrons should first be fed and then imbibe a little culture along with what was left of the wine in the bottle. I am not sure it would have worked as the waiters were to have been strategically withdrawn while we strutted and fretted for a full two hours on the platform where the orchestra normally performed. But the emergence of the Middle East as a staging point for actors is one of the phenomena of our times. In Jeddah, Muscat and Bahrein there are now caravans of actors resting in local Hiltons with free board and lodging and the use of the ballroom on three evenings a week. It is, as an enterprising impresario remarked, 'a nice change from Burnley and, of course, we are on a guarantee.'

There has been for many years a temptation for those of us with outstanding commercials or television series under our belts to go walkabout, as the Aborigines would say, in the clubs and on the stages of Australian theatres. Both the Ronnies, John Inman, Danny La Rue, Dick Emery, Harry Secombe and Molly Sugden were on the circuit this spring and many lingered on, basking in the sunshine and some vaguely reciprocal arrangement with the tax authorities. Clubs play a significant part in the Australian entertainment scene, the attraction being not so much the premises as the presence of banks of fruit machines to which the members flock at dusk like pigeons. Passion and spare cash spent they sit on, a schooner of Fosters at hand, to be consoled by visiting American pop groups or British comics, to whom the club proprietors are able to offer enormous fees. Next time casinos in this country apply for licences they should only be renewed on the promise that live entertainers will be hired along with the croupiers. Australia has the unenviable reputation of being something of an elephant's burial park for my profession, so on the whole I was rather relieved to find myself returning more or less on two legs. On the eve of my departure I lunched with Wallas Eaton – Wealthy Wal, as he was affectionately known from a long running radio series in England during the post-war years. I wanted to thank him for all the help he had been to me during the siege of *The Old Country*, not only acting in the piece rather better than I, but in explaining the text to me. An educated fellow, a friend of C. P. Snow's no less, I am afraid there is no doubt that Wallas has gone Bush. He lives on the waterside approached down a steep cliff on an inclinator, as such outside elevators are known here. We skimmed the rocky terrain over the heads of mercifully invisible red funnel (dangerous) and black widow (fatal) spiders admiring the occasional giant blue-tongued lizards and arrived safely on the terrace he has built over the ocean. Not exactly the ocean, perhaps, but the commencement of a vast inland waterway where yachtsmen and sharks bask eleven months of the year. There are not all that number of the latter apparently – more people are struck by lightning every year in Australia than get taken by them, he affirmed. But then I pointed out there is a good deal of lightning. A stab of envy urged me to try and shake him out of complacency and contemplation of the setting.

'What on earth is there to do all day?' I queried.

'I do,' he said, 'the occasional radio, the occasional television, even the occasional commercial, I do the occasional boat repair, feed the occasional koala and make the occasional new friend. I also, of course, regularly water the garden but never in my bare feet.' After lunch he conducted me to the foot of the inclinator. 'I don't think I'll come with you,' he remarked, 'It's not designed for more than one and if overloaded it does occasionally break down.' I reached the top in safety, leaving my occasional friend who may, I fear, if his misgivings about his inclinators are well founded, one day develop into the occasional hermit. I shall put him on my Christmas card list. What more can one do?

MOVABLE FEASTS

The Worldwide Gourmet

He sat beside me at the bar and, when I enquired idly about his plans, he announced he was off to Strasbourg to eat a goose. So many travellers attempt too much. His reply encapsulated a singleness of purpose altogether admirable. I don't now remember to whom I was talking, only that it was in Buck's, where such affirmations are – or at least were – listened to without distress.

How far is one prepared to go for a good meal?

I posed the question to several acquaintances. A number demanded elaboration: Do you mean a free good meal? How good is good? Myself, I would be prepared to go a long way, but then, of course, I like travelling, let alone food. Clutching my *Michelin*, how often have I sought out the rosette and crossed spoons and demanded the speciality of the house and, strangely enough, how often have I been disappointed?

There is a *Café de Paris* in Biarritz which serves, for a few golden weeks of the year, a sort of special white truffle with apples, which I found as nasty as tripe and couldn't finish. The baby lamb at *Les Beaux* is, to my mind, altogether too babyish – a veritable slaughter of the innocents – reminding me of a celebrated *restaurateur* in Gerard Street – now, alas, retired – who would explain the ritual murder necessary to prepare the feast he had in store for me. 'Mr Morley, you take a baby frog just as he utters his first bellow, and cut off his head. You must do it in the moonlight, otherwise it is no use, and then you throw away everything but the tip of the heart where the coralete is' (there was always, in the description, a word I could not catch) 'then, later, you bake this for a dozen hours on a slow peat fire, turning it over and over, and then you butter it at the table.'

'If you want a really first class moussaka,' I heard myself announce the other day, 'you'll have to go to Newbury. The fellow who was unlucky enough to be within earshot hadn't even mentioned moussaka and, as far as I know, never touched the stuff.

We each have a Gourmet Guide hidden on our person and long to expose it. 'Don't be put off by the formica tabletops,' we urge each other, 'the chef used to cook for Onassis before he took to the bottle.' We are speaking of the former chef, naturally – for we all know Aristotle was teetotal.

The impression we seek to leave is of a blue tit which has already skimmed the cream. When the milk bottle is taken inside it will not the same. The eateries we extol today will, tomorrow, be ruined by the hoi polloi – places we would not be seen dead in. 'Not quite what it was, is it?' we enquire of the still faithful customer. 'I hear the *ptarmigan à la façon de Président Giscard* is pre-cooked and frozen.' Once the hat-check girl and the diners' club take over we are off, once more, in search of the little restaurant in Shrewsbury where the firemen eat because the captain's wife comes from Bayonne and does a mincemeat tart which is out of this world.

I have two distinct approaches when eating out. Quiet confidence, as host – a hint of formality in my manner of greeting the staff. I try to impart a sense of occasion to the ritual of seating my guest and choosing the food and wine, adding a touch of originality by asking for the salt to be taken away until we have need of it. 'I don't know if you feel as I do, 'I remark to my friend, 'but I cannot bear a cruet with the aperitif.' The use of the word *cruet* here, is, I flatter myself, not without courage. Occasionally, before ordering the meal, I will summon a waiter and enquire about his wife. 'Better, I hope?' I ask him. I don't actually know whether the fellow has a wife but he will not care to correct me. He may look a little puzzled, but I am confident that my companion will mistake his bewilderment for gratitude. The impression I wish to give – and, I have no doubt, succeed in giving – is that of the late Noël Coward in charge of a happy ship: the crew's troubles are my troubles – up to a point, of course. Before choosing the wine, I always say quite simply and, indeed, truthfully, that I know nothing whatever about it. When the others have suitably expressed their disbelief, I suggest we take the wine waiter's advice. 'Something you want to get rid of,' I tell him encouragingly. 'Perhaps a Sancerre 1958, or

Sauvigny de Clos Montard '49?' I usually give a little chuckle as he departs. When he returns with the bottle I am careful not to taste it – this is a privilege I reserve for my guest.

When our roles are reversed, of course I am a totally different creature. I go for the overkill. 'What a delightful bistro!' I exclaim. 'Blue beams! I don't think I've ever seen blue beams before *and* brown paper napkins! So convenient for the Natural History Museum – it's just round the corner, surely? How did you find it? Let's stick to the set meal, shall we? It's sure to be excellent. . . I'll have what you're drinking – half a carafe will be ample. How long has this place been going?. . . And I've never heard of it. What do you suppose they're having at the next table? Who would you say the people who come here are, mostly? . . . Students? It's so jolly and unpretentious. I am reminded of a little place halfway up the Bosphorus on the right-hand side –you know it, of course – I was taken there by our Ambassador to eat yoghurt, and then we discovered this perfectly marvellous way they cook kid – in a blanket. You must try it next time you're there; just mention my name – or even the Ambassador's.'

Stored among the disorder of my memory is a positive armoury of food bombs to demolish the culinary oneupmanship of others. I always insist, for instance, that for the *millefeuilles* at the *Château de Madrid* it is worth negotiating the hairpin-bends of the Grand Corniche. 'I don't know why being circular should make all the difference,' I tell anyone who is listening, 'but somehow it does. Kobe beef in Tokyo is best, really, at the Hilton. They seem to have a particularly skilled masseur. You know that the Japanese massage the beasts on the hoof? I can't think why we don't do it here.'

No experience is too horrific to go into my book and be subsequently translated into a trap for the unwary.

The journey up-country from Bangkok to the Temple of Divine Light is seldom undertaken by train – at any rate by tourists, who prefer the river-steamer, or bus. I, on the other hand, went by rail, and have never forgotten the breakfast. I can still taste the cold fried egg, nestling in sago and topped with Soy sauce. 'Worth all the boredom of the Jade Buddha,' I maintain, stoutly. 'Be sure and catch the nine-twenty, and insist on the restaurant car.'

One of the legends of travel I like to re-tell to anyone thinking of returning from Australia by air and re-fuelling in Teheran is that, if they hasten to the Transit Lounge and take the small door on the left, next to the gentlemen's lavatory, they will find themselves at the back of the Imperial Caviare Emporium, where they have only to rouse the attendant, who sleeps under the counter, to secure enormous quantities of sturgeon roe at knock-down prices.

It may well be that the store exists, but I have not, after numerous attempts, ever discovered it. I am not sure I want to. It gives me something to look forward to on the flight.

How dull the world would be if we all knew the mystery of Glamis Castle – which reminds me of a little teashop on the left as you leave the keep, where they serve a really excellent Scotch pancake.

Just My Cup of Tea

An Englishman has the decision between tea and coffee made on his behalf right through his waking hours. The first offering is always tea, not at breakfast which is taken later and accompanied by coffee in the better class home. Class is what coffee and tea are all about. Coffee is up market, advertised by top people like David Niven, tea is shown on the television screen as being the beverage more suitable to the needs of chimpanzees and army personnel below the rank of officer. But a cup of early morning tea, especially when brought to the bedside by staff trained to place the tray noiselessly on the bedside table and with a few slices of brown bread and butter cut wafer thin to accompany the brew, is acceptable. If you insist on drinking tea at breakfast, it has to be China tea, the Indian mixture is frowned upon along with the bacon sandwiches. There *are* people who drink Indian tea to start their day but with any luck these will be gainfully employed and thus out of sight on the factory floor long before you yourself are up and about. Nor will the fact that they will be interrupting their work by drinking it out of thick mugs continuously for the next eight hours or so worry you unless you are their employer or a business efficiency expert.

Tea drinking in Britain is as much of a ceremony as it is in Japan but our teacups are larger. The workers have won the right not only to sip it continuously while on the job, but to adjourn for lengthy periods during the day to concentrate on what are called tea breaks. Sometimes they visit temples known as canteens, sometimes the temple comes in to them in the form of a movable altar or trolley containing not only the tea urn itself but an offering of sticky buns, meat pies and fancy cakes which are sold at bargain prices to the faithful, unless you happen to be entertaining them on your own premises when they will not expect to pay for anything. Builders, plumbers, telephone engineers, men calling to repair the television are offered tea immediately upon arrival and afterwards at approximately twenty-minute intervals. Sweet and strong is how they like it. Sweet and strong, you vainly hope they will remain but this is not a likely occurrence. The British workman tires easily and needs constant encouragement of a 'cuppa' along with the provision of telephone and bathroom facilities if he is to remain happy and contented on your premises; indeed if he is to remain there at all.

On the other hand there is no such thing as a coffee break for the higher paid worker or executive whose coffee is brought to him at his desk by his secretary at regular intervals until lunchtime. His last cup of coffee will be partaken at some fashionable restaurant after luncheon and he will then try to arrive back at his office in time for a cup of tea while he signs his letters and arranges for his car to be brought round from the car park in order to get home before the traffic becomes heavy.

Because coffee is supposed to stimulate the consumer for the task ahead, a cup is usually offered any visitor before getting down to the purpose of the visit. It is considered good manners to apologize for the quality of the mix which is wont to arrive in a plastic cup. Gone are the days when anyone in the country cared to grind a coffee bean himself, let alone roast it. Only very occasionally across a crowded pavement there wafts towards you the scent of a bean being readied for consumption but not, alas, for you who will have to be content with the substitute coffee powder spooned from a paper bag, all freshness, aroma and taste long since departed.

It is the Englishman's love of animals that causes such prodigious consumption of coffee and tea in our land. Trained as we are from birth to putting down saucers of milk and biscuits at regular intervals on the kitchen floor for our domestic pets, it is not long before we adopt the habit of perpetually sipping and munching ourselves. We do not, however, lap and gobble at speed; indeed many advertisements for the human dog biscuit emphasize the time taken to munch on the caramel filling. There is money available for the inventor of the custard cream with the chewing gum centre.

Coffee is supposed, as we have noted earlier, to stimulate the thought process. Preliminary coffee is mandatory before an actor rehearses, a committee approves the minutes of their last meeting or negotiations on a wage settlement can commence. On the other hand, tea is strictly reserved to minimize catastrophe. Survivors of train crashes, pedestrians knocked flying on zebra crossings and policemen hit on the head by flying brickbats are traditionally rewarded with a cup, as indeed are all those whom we consider are due for a shock. 'You are not going to believe this,' we warn them, 'so sit down and have a cup of tea before we tell you what's happened.' In vain for the patient to demand to get it over and done with. Once the kettle has boiled, we stand over him until he has drained the cup before we inform him that his car has been stolen or he has been declared redundant. Either way we join him in a second cup.

Don't Drink the Water

I have always had a nose for food, by which I mean if I am set down in the middle of a foreign city which I have never visited before and turned round three times I can generally manage to lead my companions to a good restaurant. Of course, they are not to know that if I had set off in the opposite direction from the one I chose we might all have been sitting down sooner. But there are signs and portents to be observed. The name can be important. If it can be roughly translated as the Smugglers' Rest or the Cracked Lobster I seldom venture inside. I look for discreet side streets along which one light burns from a doorway and a line of sleek motor cars parked some distance away. The make of the car is important, a vintage specimen among them or a chauffeur hunched at the wheel and you may press on with all convenient speed. If the restaurant is already full but the head waiter suggests that you have a drink at the bar and one will soon be vacant, resist the invitation. In my experience people do not gulp their coffee, call for the bill, cram on their hats and coats and leap for the exit just because I am standing at the bar waiting to be fed. They should, but they don't. Waiting for tables causes frustration, a sense of deprivation and eventually heartburn. You cannot be entirely sure whether the other patrons are being seated out of turn, as the evening draws on, you have had a surfeit of salted almonds and sense that you are no longer as welcome as you thought. Dinner when it is served had better be worth the wait, you tell yourself, and, alas, seldom is.

Montreal is a city which prides itself on its cooking, there is a whole *quartier* given over to olde worlde bistro style nosh. Pot au feu, red cabbage and white sausage, Normandy pancakes, Mediterranean *bouillabaisse* – but I resisted the obvious choices and after a search came upon the Iroquois which still serves buffalo meat and Indian bread, molasses and hazelnuts cooked in the fashion of the Mohahawk tribe. I made up my mind to eat buffalo more often. If you can imagine a goose crossed with a hind you get some idea of the taste. I suppose really one shouldn't eat buffalo. Like the human race it is almost certainly by now an endangered species. I often tell myself I should have been a vegetarian like the journalist who came to interview me this week. He was into meditation, judo, a Chinese system for learning the violin when one reaches the age of three combined with a deep sense of obligation to the Lord Buddha with one day a week devoted to repaying him with devotional studies. He seemed a good deal better adjusted and altogether lighter on his feet than I and had an almost magical approach to fellow motorists. 'Do you think they mind you cutting in quite so often?' I asked. But he seemed satisfied that under the protection of the faith he was creating no fresh problems for the non-believers. He told me Buddhism was the most rapidly growing religion in the world today and with the possible exception of slaughtermen embraced all walks of life. He made me aware, if I wasn't so already, of the alternative approach to life and particularly food.

Why am I such a 'stick in the steak and chips'? Half the world doesn't eat enough and the rest of us too much – yet, try as I may, I cannot go overboard about rice and bean shoots, fresh seaweed or caraway seed. I have tried them often enough, goodness knows, but however genuine the ambience, however sparse the surroundings, I suspend belief. Surely, I tell myself, this is not how raw tuna fish should taste, voicing my doubts once in Aberdeen – not the one in Scotland but the one to which most Aberdonians go to make their fortune, Hong Kong. On the malodorous water front formidable Chinese grandmothers wait to ferry you across to the floating restaurants where the food is nothing like so good as in Brewer Street. 'It's a long way to come for rubbish,' I told the waiter, and an elderly Mandarin at the next table sympathizing with my protest led me back over the junks and eventually to what I imagine must be the ultimate Chinchinese restaurants where we joined a private party of the *cognoscenti* and prepared to feast. I don't know how many courses were served during the marathon – I lost count at about ten – but I do know that except for fabalone with which the proceedings commenced we concentrated on duck, roasted, flattened, squeezed, pancaked, stewed, minced and curried, drawn and quartered. We finally consumed the webbing between the toes and I think possibly the beak. At the end, a steaming cauldron of duck soup was set in front of me. It was a long time before I could once again contemplate the creatures in or out of the Serpentine.

For some years I was retained by one of my children as a food critic for a weekly magazine and, when he finally retired me, I became an inspector of restaurants for a prestigious American travel guide. Over the brandy I would make surreptitious and, alas, as I discovered the next morning, indecipherable notes on the menu. I learnt to go for the chefs – by which I don't mean attack them but find out the sort of people they were. Chefs are infinitely more fascinating than the food they cook. I had a friend who made a point of inviting the most renowned of them to stay with him and because he was a millionaire they accepted. He made one condition that during their stay they should cook a meal for him on the premises. 'What distinguished them from us mortals,' he told me, 'is that they all kept their hats on in the kitchen and never touched the gas taps once they had turned them up.'

Cooking, like acting, is all a question of confidence. The most confident cooks in the world, but by no means the best, are the French. I have yet to meet the proprietor of the humblest *estaminet* who admitted to a mistake by one of his employees. The customer is always wrong. On the other hand a Russian will gladly remove any dish from under the nose of a complaining customer but the way service is in Russian restaurants you will be lucky if you are given another chance. If you don't want to eat it, they indicate, there are plenty who do. With the Russians you are back in the nursery. Only with the Italians does cheerfulness prevail and Italian food is still the best and cheapest in the West. Even if you do not care too much for the first mouthful, by the time they have added the cheese and ground the black peppers and laid on the Chianti, you begin to enjoy yourself and by the time they have served the glass of sambuca and lit the coffee bean floating on top, you, too, are usually aglow.

Most holidays start and end with the plastic tray compartmentalized with the fast food and the complimentary half-bottle of plonk. The whole thing is complimentary in a sense and as one tackles the trifle on the outward journey one looks forward to the richer delights in store on the morrow by the bathing pool. Coming home one is often grateful for the sensible ham sandwich and reassured by the British Airways tea pot.

Time was when the food on trains was better but that time is past. The catering on most is sparse and expensive. No exception is the

Canadian Pacific Mainline Express over the Rockies or the Trans-Siberian Railway, unless you happen to strike the caviare before it disappears with amazing speed down the throats of Australian students who have finally succeeded in finding customers for their safari caravans after months of hanging around the National Car Park outside the National Theatre.

The French have given up, the Spaniards never started, only the German trains serve good meals with the possible exceptions of the Thais and their elaborate breakfasts out of Bangkok on the way to the Bridge on the River Kwai and the Silver Buddha—which brings us back more or less where we started and my friendly journalist who plucked ripe apricots from the trees as he trudged the plains of Tibet and contracted dysentery.

'What did you do then?' I asked.

'Kept walking,' he told me. 'The choice was a simple one, as is usually the way with Buddha – either I struggled on or lay down and died.'

When my generation was young it was taught never to drink the water. The world has grown smaller, more crowded and lethal. Next time I go on a package holiday to Lhasa I shall take my own package of dried fruits.

THE SILVER SCREEN

The Human Factor

'I do not understand what the feathers are for.' Mr Otto Preminger removes his eye from the view-finder and regards the property master in sorrow with a hint of anger.

'They are pens, quill pens,' he is told by that long-suffering individual. 'We need to wait until you have dressed the set.'

Waiting is the cardinal sin, whoever causes the delay is guilty of a grave dereliction of duty unless, of course, it is Otto himself. 'I do not understand,' he will tell Richard Attenborough, 'why you are not here, I have had to call you seven times.'

'Once,' Attenborough tells him, 'and I was just outside the door.'

'Outside the door is no good for me.'

I don't know what made filming *The Human Factor* such a pleasing experience, or rather I know very well. Preminger has the effect Churchill must have had on people. Beneath his stern, sometimes forbidding exterior, you glimpse genuine irresponsibility. Shall I, I asked myself, in the first day's shooting remonstrate when shouted at to keep quiet. It was, after all, Otto who was making the din. 'I am sorry,' I rehearsed my protest silently to myself. 'I am sorry, Otto, but unless everyone is kind and patient I cannot act properly.' I suspected the reply might involve my instant dismissal and kept my mouth shut for once. The scene played better than I expected.

Otto quite often tells actors to go if they're not happy. Nicol Williamson took him at his word and walked off the set pursued for once by an abject Otto. After all, his leading man was halfway through the picture. The great Gabriel Pascal sacked his star in *Major Barbara* after three weeks and reshot the entire film up to then with Rex Harrison playing the part but then Gabriel had not much sense of money. Otto on the other hand is not one to waste the pennies. He signs every cheque each Friday himself, enquiring thoughtfully about the overtime charges and, on a film such as this one, the employees number well over a hundred. His approach to actors is uncompromising, either they know the lines or they don't. Where other directors chop and change Otto sets up the camera and presses forward. Artistes who expect to cover their mistakes in close-ups are usually disappointed. He is the only director I ever worked with who tires of the scene before the actor does.

Long after the anger has gone out of his eyes he will continue staring at some luckless extra whose attention has momentarily wandered or has spoken out of turn. 'Have you never opened a door?' he will thunder at one of his cast newly arrived on the set. 'I find it extraordinary that you should come to my picture and not be able to open a door.' Here the moment of decision occurs; if the actor remonstrates, expresses his own belief that he has indeed opened doors before – the battle is lost. He will be accused of cheating, of wasting time, even of sabotage. If, on the other hand, he watches while Otto himself manipulates the knob, subsequently expressing his gratitude and pleasure at having one of life's little mysteries explained to him, he will have joined the club and quite possibly not be shouted at again for the whole morning. If and when he ever retires from directing, Mr Preminger should be preserved with a magnificent grant from the industry and required to train young actors to stand up for themselves as men, and to instruct horses intended for riot control to accustom themselves to shouting and the waving of flags.

If I have observed anything about the business of making motion pictures it is that over the years robustness has departed. Film actors grow lethargic when stroked with kid gloves, they are at their best when goaded beyond endurance and are about to lose control. Preminger keeps them perplexed and often resentful. The racehorse allowed to proceed at his own pace seldom wins the race. Before filming *The Human Factor* I had spent a month shooting another script in the gardens of the Huntingdon Library, a blissful experience with a director of immense charm and patience who listened courteously to every actor in turn and, however idiotic the suggestion, appeared to consider it seriously even though seldom adopting it, faced with a company of comedians all of whom including myself thought we were a good deal funnier than the script. His patience was inexhaustible as the strawberries and cream which he arranged to have served to us along with the cooling drinks and the quite exceptional buffet luncheons.

The only creatures who seemed dissatisfied with the proceedings were a number of exceptionally un-cooperative ostriches whom I have an uneasy feeling will almost certainly steal the picture. I don't say I acted better for Preminger but without the cream teas I certainly tried harder to do so. Actors who achieve any sort of eminence learn to soak up flattery like a sponge. In their determination to remain unspoiled and totally without conceit they grow into the dullest people imaginable. Preminger is guiltless of such corruption, he lavishes little praise, expresses the lowest level of appreciation consistent with good manners – for he remains off the set and even occasionally on camera, a profoundly courteous man. Along with his Austrian accent he has maintained a mid-European sense of style, he has a beautiful wife and two good-looking sons who came over while he was filming on a promise of tickets to Wimbledon. Another son, he informed me proudly, was born out of wedlock and is currently engaged on a book about his distinguished mother Gipsy Rose Lee. I don't know if he still goes home to the cream cakes at Deml's and the Lippizaner Horses, the Horn of the Unicorn and the Hotel Sacher. But it's nice to know he is alive and well, even if he doesn't live in Vienna any longer.

Western Reproaches

Someone had thoughtfully tuned the television to a repeat of *Upstairs, Downstairs,* set out the ice bucket with the champagne on top of the set along with the gin bottle, the tonics and fresh limes, and in a moment the limo (for we are in America, gentle readers) had left the normally rigorously-maintained No Parking bay, where it had been standing for at least a half-hour outside Los Angeles airport, and we were on our way – albeit at no great speed.

Limos, in common with Canadian Pacific railway engines, as I was to discover later, have no great turn of foot especially, in the former case, when they are conveying not only freshly-opened champagne but unidentifiable VIPs cloistered and sustained behind opaque glass windows.

We drove for a few miles along what I mistook for a tunnelled motorway and I was just congratulating the Los Angeles authorities on constructing so formidable an underground link between Los Angeles Airport and Beverly Hills when I realized that we were indeed out in the open, but that through the glass roof only one star's reflection could be glimpsed.

Lest I give the impression that I am accustomed to maintaining the lifestyle of Barbra Streisand, I must point out that the circumstances were somewhat exceptional in so much that advertising British Airways in America, a task with which I have been entrusted for some time, is now the joint responsibility of myself and the prestigiously titled firm of Foote, Cone and Belding, who are comparative newcomers to the account. In a media phrase, we have switched agencies.

Whoever was responsible for pushing the limo out was not, of course, Mr Foote, Mr Cone or Mr Belding himself, all of them have long since retired from the firm which proudly bears their names. Only

Mr Cone is still a surviving father figure in the industry, and credited with having awakened American palates to the realization that gum cleans as it chews as it sweetens. Besides capturing the British Airways account, the agency had also entrapped a pristine copywriter who, although conducting himself with the superb modesty hitherto only exhibited by myself, had recently been responsible for almost the entire American nation withdrawing their funds from other banking houses, and indeed from under their mattresses, and entrusting them to the establishment for which he coined (and I make no excuse for the pun) the immortal slogan 'You worked hard for your money and we do the same'.

Even so, he had quite a job persuading me to carry on the shoot a furled umbrella which, at a touch on the handle, displayed a Union Jack normally secreted in the ferrule. 'It is an insult to the flag,' I told him, 'principally because I am clumsy.' Actually it often needed a good deal more than a touch but time passes pleasantly enough on these occasions and over yet more champagne I learned that another member of the talent, as we actors are referred to, was not only the sister-in-law of the late Cedric Hardwicke but had been a member of the court of Louis XVI (never quite sure of the number) when I had essayed the role on the very same lot at Culver City precisely forty-two years earlier. Survival is the name of the game.

My task completed, and with no more champagne immediately in prospect, I thought I might fulfil a lifelong ambition to ride the Canadian Pacific Railway across the Rockies to Montreal, where I planned further exposure in a film supporting Benji, a likeable mongrel who was already there, shooting his latest film, *A Heavenly Dog*. Alas, the journey was not all that it is cracked up to be and I can only advise would-be fellow travellers to wait until spring for the clouds to clear, the snow to melt and an occasional mountain peak to be glimpsed. By the time Calgary was reached I had had enough of leaden skies and leaden food in the dining-car and flew. If I have a further word of useful advice to fellow explorers, remember to travel with a plug for the wash basin. In Montreal I found Omar Sharif eagerly awaiting my arrival at the Blue Bonnets, which is not, as you might imagine knowing him, a go-go disco or a bridge club, but the local race-track where he kept open house and his own private stock of caviare, entertaining members of the cast and crew and any jockey under temporary suspension who cared to mark his card.

The evenings seemed to pass in a flash but the days took longer.

Although I hesitate to decry a fellow artiste, Benji is not the most reliable of performers and, like myself, seemed to have only the haziest idea of what the story was about. His trainer, a patient fellow who had once trained a pig not only to turn on the television but subsequently to watch the programme, and had started his career with Rin Tin Tin, was constantly producing small pieces of steak and a live guinea pig to attract his attention and sustain his interest.

'He doesn't want to eat the guinea pig, does he?' I asked.

'No, no,' explained Frank, 'they adore each other; he fulfils the same function as a goat in the stall of a racehorse. Benji gets bored with only human company.'

On the days I was not needed to display my trouser legs and speak my lines just as I judged Benji to be about on his marks, I was free to wander about Montreal and sample the cooking of this enclave of France where the authorities insist that nothing shall be written in English which hasn't been displayed first in French and the paperwork thereby created is every bit as time-consuming as the Value Added Tax is at home.

When the time came for me to leave, I sought out Benji who, his role completed for the day, was dozing happily in a crowded *café chantant*, where brunch was being served to the accompaniment of wandering minstrels and two young ladies in the guise of clowns executing an incomprehensible mime show with invisible bubble gum.

'Just came to say *au revoir*, old chap,' I told him as he solemnly extended a paw.

'You haven't signed his autograph book,' they reminded me, and I wrote over my name: 'Thank Heaven For Little Dogs' and gave him the last of my steak.

If the Face Fits

Lady Lucan's complaint that the actor engaged to play her husband in a forthcoming documentary on the BBC doesn't add up in her book to a nobleman, and in any case lacks the necessary Slav blood, drew a sharp reply from Mr Tony Matthews. 'I do not think,' he is quoted as saying, 'that "yob" is a fair description. After all, I was head prefect of an English public school.' The mother of the murdered nanny is similarly dissatisfied with the choice of the actress to play her daughter and suggested that although filming is almost completed, the BBC would be wise to switch the two leading ladies in the documentary reconstruction of the crime, thereby at least ensuring accuracy of hair colouring. The whole controversy pinpoints the difficulties experienced by members of my profession when called upon to portray real-life characters in the historical or contemporary context.

I remember the comment of the playwright's mother when viewing my own interpretation of Oscar Wilde: 'A walking stick is not going to help in the leading role.' Like most actors of my girth, I have been asked from time to time to impersonate Winston Churchill. Mr Timothy West recently succumbed to the temptation and succeeded where others (with the possible exception of Mike Yarwood) have failed. He wasn't Churchill, but he was very like Churchill might have been if he had been Mr West. Compromise is the secret. In my time I collected my share of regal roles, usually from MGM and usually French about whom the public knows little; but I did once essay the mad father of the Prince Regent and got the mad bit so right that the present monarch, who had been forced to watch me in my nightshirt setting fire to the Windsor Castle organ, decided that thereafter her appearance at Royal Command film performances was by no means to be taken for granted.

Actors engaged to play Landru, Wilberforce, Paton or Hugh

Gaitskell always profess themselves (at the outset, at any rate) delighted with the task ahead. Often they go to extreme lengths, carrying photographs of the character with them to prop up on the make-up table, prior to assuming the necessary disguise.

Traditional roles are often the easiest: Napoleon's method of resting his elbow, King Richard's rounded shoulder, Nelson's eye-patch and missing arm are cake-walks compared to the problems confronting actors engaged to depict Shakespeare or John D. Rockefeller. In earlier times the late George Arliss and Anna Neagle triumphed by the simple expedient of being themselves and daring the public to argue. Of course Queen Victoria, Nurse Cavell and Odette looked and spoke like Anna, and Disraeli, Rothschild and Wellington were the spitting image of George, although it was rumoured that Miss Neagle in her portrayal of the Queen Empress chewed cotton wool in the final scenes.

My own most successful historical interpretation was that of the Earl of Manchester in the film *Cromwell*; by the time I had got round to securing for myself a role in this epic all the plums seemed to have fallen or been gathered by other actors who subscribed to the *Film Weekly*. I came late on the scene, and having discovered that the film was casting one morning, found myself by tea-time interviewing Irving Allen the producer. He leafed through the available vacancies and offered Manchester. I was surprised to find that there was such a city in those days, even more that it should have possessed an Earl. However, as he was still on the tree I picked him with alacrity, and was relieved to discover that the researcher had not got round to deciding what His Grace would have looked like, and that there was therefore no necessity for me to disguise my features. Nothing is more conducive to comfort on film locations than not having to arrive at daybreak to affix a beard or stick on a wig.

In point of fact, I seem to remember that Manchester did wear the latter, but under a hat and it was the hat which saved the day as far as I was concerned: a wide-brimmed felt affair with feathers, supplying the necessary resemblance to *Puss-in-Boots*. I took enormous pains to keep the feathers dry, enclosing them in cellophane, often in shot and on the battlefields provided the enemy and camera were not too close. For the first few days I mounted a horse, but whereas the other nobles rode at full gallop I proceeded at a nervous walk. Spanish film horses (and the film was shot mostly in Spain) are trained not only to stop at a tug of the rein but then to gently keel over backwards, and it was to avoid this hazardous display of equine sagacity that I let the reins hang loose and hoped the creature understood he must stop before actually knocking down the director. Life became easier when I was transferred to a coach after my horse had once literally sunk from under me in a bog during a prolonged close-up.

There were not many close-ups available to Manchester; my role consisted chiefly of pinpointing the location for the various battlefields.

'Where are we?' I would bellow as I alighted nervously from my carriage.

'Edgbaston, Sire' or 'Marston Moor,' came the helpful reply and I and the public were thus able to catch up with history.

I was equally fortunate in my portrayal of the Emperor of China in the film of *Genghis Khan*, perhaps even more than I deserved. Arriving on the second evening of the night location in Yugoslavia, and somewhat behind time, I dispensed with the Chinese pallor and elaborate eye-shading and took my place among the hordes confident that my Caucasian characteristics would be undetected in the general scrum. Alas, the rain started, the cameras moved in, and I waited for the inevitable storm to break and the displeasure of all concerned to be manifested during an hour's delay while my features were corrected. Nothing of the kind occurred, and I almost completed my role in the picture as the first all-white Chinese Emperor with the occasional addition of elongated fingernails. On the very last day, however, and by this time in Berlin, the management engaged a crowd of genuine Chinese concubines with which to surround me and I successfully persuaded the director to allow me to stand at some distance from such implied debauchery.

So my advice to the cast of *Carry On Up the Zambesi*, or whatever this particular Lucan BBC epic is titled, is not to visit Madame Tussaud's, supposing the noble Earl and his entourage have already arrived there, but to play the roles as to the manner born, insisting that the film credits make it perfectly clear which character they are sustaining. Years and years ago, led out to the scaffold as Louis XVI on the vast set constructed by MGM for the filming of *Marie Antoinette*, I remember the proceedings being momentarily halted by the last desperate efforts of the historical researcher to draw the director's attention to the more blatant anomalies in the sets. Glancing at the historical engravings of the scene clutched in the hand of the elderly researcher, the great director Woody Van Dyke remarked sagely: 'Kid! That's how it was, but this is how it's going to be!'

THE HAPPY PUNTER

Keeping an Eye on the Pressure

Department stores are now installing machines which, when rewarded with a 50p coin, will tell you how your blood pressure is coming along. Readers may remember that, when the time came for the tripod camera and the gentleman dodging around under the black hood finally to go out of business, they were replaced with a curtained booth, a confession box furnished not with a grill behind which hid a candid priest, but a candid camera which gave you up to a dozen or so alternative faces in a very short time.

There is a good deal of resistance among the medical profession to this latest toy. If there is one thing doctor's don't encourage it's a do-it-yourself kit for the patient. We'll take the blood pressure, the urine sample, we'll do the tapping and the sounding if you don't mind and often, of course, if you do.

There is a good reason for a doctor to cling to his stethoscope and his blood pressure gauge, and to rap his ice cold knuckles around the region of your liver. Quite simply it gives him, does it not, something to do while he is racking his brains to think of what on earth is the matter with you.

You have already told him that and demanded a bottle of tonic whose name you have forgotten but which did you a power of good when you got back from that holiday in Bournemouth in '63, or just possibly'64. I believe one shook the bottle, you tell him, otherwise there was sedimentation. Bitter lemon, he suggests, while undoing that dreadful little black box, taking out the inflatable bandage, and fixing it far too tightly around your arm.

Let's just have a look at your blood pressure, he suggests, taking care to angle the dial out of your vision. Now he starts telling you about his recent holiday in the Lake District and squeezes the rubber ball.

The bandage tightens before he releases a screw and regards the apparatus with considerable suspicion. Once is never enough. While he is waiting for the mercury or whatever to settle, he will usually ask a rather personal question. Do you get up in the night or have much trouble climbing stairs?

You realize he has left Windermere, is no longer retasting the barbecue spare ribs his eldest child cooked unaided over the primus, and is back in business. You attempt not to add to his anxiety which has palpably risen along with the reading, and at the same time to stop your own heart from pounding. I usually take the lift, you tell him, or, not since I knocked off the Ovaltine you recommended last time.

Soon he is back again pumping and looking at you with some dismay. Then with a sigh he disengages the bandage and packs up the box. It's up, he tells you. It always is when anyone takes it, you tell him, beginning to feel calmer and hoping he will. Of course, in your case, he volunteers, struggling to look on the bright side, you do have rather a large arm. Is that bad, you ask? It's bad in some ways with an arm like yours, you sometimes get a rather exaggerated reading; yours is high all the same.

At this point he volunteers two numbers one of which is mysteriously over the other. About the tonic, you suggest, I have a feeling it had strychnine in it. What you need, he replies, is to lose some weight. We are back to square one but the black box is now back in the drawer. You may or may not get the tonic but you are almost certain to be landed with a diet sheet and some appetite depressant pills.

It was, therefore, with a feeling of optimism that I found myself in the men's outfitting department of my friendly neighbourhood store, optimism speedily dispelled by a large poster proclaiming 'Blood Pressure, the Silent Killer'. Among the supporting credits I read that blood pressure damages the blood vessels, heart, kidneys and brain.

A young lady in the garb of a nurse stood hopefully by a kind of pin table willing to accept the 50p which was needed for a contest and, if necessary, give change. Sit down, she urged kindly, and let your arm rest lightly in the clamp but first, she suggested, take off your jacket. And shirt, I asked? Good heavens no, with this machinery it is not even necessary to roll up your shirt sleeve. My, I told her, how science jumps ahead.

It was then I realized that blood pressure testing is a spectator sport. Just as in Las Vegas men and women hang around the one-arm bandits to observe the play and step in themselves when they judge the jackpot imminent, so the machine when in action draws a small body of dedicated onlookers who wait with bated breath for the score to be recorded in bold red numbers.

For a time the numbers were not forthcoming but the space where they were to finally appear carried a message that all was well and that the examination was continuing. Finally released from the gentle embrace of the inflatable bandage, I was able to read the dreaded score. I glanced down quickly at the table which displayed the acceptable systolic and diastolic pressures. No one had ever explained this mystery before but any satisfaction I felt at mastering the system was immediately dispelled by the realization that my own reading were quite unacceptable.

At this point the lady in charge handed me a small blue folder on which was inscribed. 'My Personal Life Saving Account' under which was printed the general reference chart for adults. On the back she had filled in my vital statistics for the morning. There were ten black spaces for further readings and underneath instructions for calculating my average blood pressure. 'Calculate your average blood pressure,' it read, 'by adding each column and dividing each by the total number of measurements.'

'I learnt all that at school,' I told her gleefully.

'Are you,' she asked, 'consulting a doctor?'

'Pretty well all the time.'

I lingered by the Vita Stat, reading my new credentials.

'It says here,' I chided, 'that I should have raised the left arm overhead, rapidly opening and closing my hand for thirty seconds, no wonder I got such a poor reading.'

'Would you like to try again?'

'Let someone else have a go.'

I noticed that my higher than average score was still recorded in figures of blood.

'Does it stay there until someone else puts in 50 pence?'

'Or till we turn off the machine,' she told me.

'I find it rather embarrassing. For heaven's sake, let's get someone else involved.'

'It's very slack for a Tuesday,' she said, but just then a man I judged to be an *habitué* approached, briskly inserted a coin and after a minute or so came up with an even higher score than mine.

Immeasurably relieved, I took over from Nurse.

'Are you seeing your doctor?' I asked.

'Of course,' he told me. 'And taking three tablets of reserpine a day. The joke is I am a pharmaceutical salesman based in Switzerland.'

'That must be a good business,' I said.

'We don't make the profits we once did. I shall have to increase the dose.'

'That should put up the profits.'

'Not one of our products,' he told me sadly, and wandered away.

'Wasn't he nervous?' said my colleague in the cap and apron.

'Tell me,' I asked, 'what did you do before this?'

Apparently, like me, she had worked for British Airways.

'What made you take this up?'

'It makes a change.'

In all fairness I must record she had trained at St. George's.

I turned to find a friend regarding me with curiosity.

'What on earth are you doing?' she asked. 'I thought you hated shopping.'

'Let me,' I begged, 'treat you to a blood pressure test.'

'I'd certainly like to sit down,' she told me, but a few minutes later she obviously wished she hadn't.

'Are you seeing a doctor?' I asked.

'I felt perfectly all right before you made that absurd suggestion.'

'It's not nearly as high as mine,' I said.

'Wait here,' she told me. 'When I have bought a skirt, you can take me out for a gin and tonic.'

She disappeared and again we were alone. Emboldened and anxious to fill in the time I asked a very smart lady *en route* for the escalator whether she would allow me to stand her a reading.

'Not likely,' she told me. 'I've had three coronaries already.'

We chatted amicably about Greece, whither she at last persuaded her physician to let her fly for Christmas. She was, it transpired, a lecturer on philosophy.

The only other customer to appear was a stout party burdened with Christmas shopping. She seemed to understand the machine better than we did, scored a faultless reading and hurried away.

My fellow spectators were obviously puzzled. 'I quite thought,' murmured one of them who turned out to be an employee hoping in vain for an eyesight test, 'she'd be way up.'

My friend reappeared and we went in search of a pub.

'There is very little a gin and tonic can't cure,' I told her. 'If you're good, I may give you a Lumi Tronic Mark III for Christmas. It's the home version of the Vita Stat. Then when your friends call you can take their blood pressure before and after the brandy.'

'I can't afford to give them brandy,' she told me.

For my part, I certainly couldn't afford to give her a Lumi Tronic.

Death of a Snailsman

The death of the man reputed to be the most successful snail trainer in the world highlights once again the danger of competitive sport. There is, thank goodness, no shortage of men and women still prepared to face fearful odds. And the late Mr Hudson was certainly no ordinary snail trainer, as visitors to his extensive snail stud and training establishment just outside East Grinstead will bear witness.

I have never forgotten the first time he invited me to 'Slimetrails', the lovely country house which adjoined his paddocks. Trophies, photographs and shells covered the walls of every room in the house while in his own office I even spied several privileged ex-champions crawling on the ceiling. Indeed, one actually fell into my coffee cup as he passed it across the desk.

'With or without?' he remarked cheerfully while he extracted the creature expertly with finger and thumb and transferred him to his blotter. 'He will probably dry out this time,' he assured me. 'Snails have a natural sense of self preservation but I am afraid Perce Agincourt III is getting a bit old for that sort of caper. Perce won the Cheltenham Grand Prix way back in '74; I made a packet that day,' he confided. 'Came in at eight to one backed down from fourteens.'

He stirred his own coffee and gently propelled Perce a few inches. After a shock like that, he informed me, they must be kept moving.

'Tell me,' he asked, 'what do you want to know?'

'Everything,' I told him. 'How did it all start?'

'Well, I suppose I was ten when I first decided to become a snail racing trainer. Father wasn't too keen at first. He was a window-cleaner himself and kept pigeons so it's in the blood I suppose, but it was my mother who really encouraged me not to follow Dad with the old chamois and the step-ladder. Mind you, it's a good business, even today, mostly cash, but I never fancied heights particularly after Dad had his fall and had to go around on crutches. Mother thought I would be safer on the ground and so it proved – mind you, this game is not without risks, it's the travelling really.

'Snails have got something we humans haven't. They never try to go too fast or too far. That's what makes the sport so fascinating although, mind you, I once had a fellow who could do 50 yards in 16 minutes flat. But I could never win a race with him – wonderful on the home gallops but when he saw another snail near him he refused to budge, even in the mating season. I often thought he must be a bit bent but when I entered him in cobbler races it was the same story.'

'Cobblers?' I queried.

'Cobblers are the same as colts before they've been cut, of course. Mind you, you only cut a snail if he plays up. Never had to cut old Perce here and look at him now. Fit as a flea though not so active as he used to be. Still, he looks as if he's recovered. I'll just put him back on the ceiling, and then I expect you'd like to look around.'

'What does he eat up there?' I asked.

'Nothing, he comes down for his tea,' he told me. 'Bran and lettuce, that's what they all get. Snails will eat anything except garlic, you know. Natural I suppose – they get a sort of foreboding about garlic. Cruel stuff, I always think.'

'Do you ever eat them?' I asked.

'Do horse trainers eat horses?' he replied. 'Well, they do in France you might say, but not in this country, thank heavens.' Outside he introduced me to one of his assistants. 'This is Fred, he looks after the walls and the gallops. You have to keep both in tip-top condition, that's the secret or one of them. The others are training and especially breeding.'

He took me to see the snail nurseries, delicate little crustaceans following their parents around the small, well-kept lawns in front of the breeding pens. Each enclosure, I noted, had its own individual plunge pool.

'They don't do better than this in Vegas,' my host assured me. 'It's important they should learn to swim as soon as possible, best thing for their muscles. At six months the training begins in earnest.'

He took me over to where half a dozen pretty girls in breeches and boots were each concentrating on drawing a plastic lettuce leaf gently across the sward pursued by one of their charges.

'Keep it straight, lass. Hold it there, let him get a sniff, right, off you go, reckon that one's had enough, rub him down and put him back in his stall.'

For each girl he had an encouraging word of advice but his eyes, I noticed, never left the shells and their occupants.

'Sometimes,' he confided, 'we do have to go in for a bit of lemon on their tails – seems to sting them up. Start them off. Mind you, none of that on the tracks, they have to do without the lettuce and the lemon, except in Miami for some reason. The authorities there allow it.

'The real trouble,' he confided later back in his den, over a whisky and soda into which he occasionally dipped his fingers and moistened Perce Agincourt III's antlers, now waiting for his tea, 'the real trouble is keeping the owners happy. Mind you, it costs a bit to keep a snail in training and then, as I mentioned before, there's the travelling expenses. If they're keen they like to come and see for themselves. Luckily the prize money is getting bigger all the time. Then there's sponsorship. The garden fertilizer firms are beginning to come in. You must excuse me now, I have my race entries to make. The European telephones are the very devil but you can say one thing about the sport. It's clean, we don't have any bloody jockeys in this game, thank God, not yet anyway!'

The Christmas Air Raid

For some of us Christmas is an air raid from which we long to take cover. I've had seventy Christmases and seventy Christmas dinners, although the first was a bit sparse. The temptation of crouching under the staircase becomes annually stronger. That's not to say I don't love the family and the decorations and the presents and the visit of a very dear old friend who stipulates transport back to the Smoke on Boxing Day not later than five. Besides I'm the head of the family now since Gladys Cooper died, and there are responsibilities and the privilege of not having to carve the bird – not that I ever did. Delegate is the secret, let someone else lay the table and bring in the logs. In our house there are always willing hands – my wife's. By Christmas Eve she's absolutely exhausted. What if I were to go away next year – what if we both were to do so? There are hotels in Torquay which others patronize. The festivities are subdued and, even if they become embarrassingly hearty, there is the bedroom and even better the bed. Dangerous thoughts, it could happen sooner than I think. 'I'll just take the tray up to Grandfather, perhaps I'll try and get him to pull a cracker.' No, but before then, the atmosphere of the Grand Hotel, elderly incumbents dining quietly alone, pulling their cracker with the head waiter taking care he gets the paper crown. Or I suppose I could do something useful like scurrying around a hospital ward or relieving a traffic warden. Christmas is shorter for actors if they're working, two performances on Boxing Day, in New York two performances on Christmas Day itself. I suppose it's shorter too for priests, skeleton shift workers and Safari Park attendants.

For most of us it's long enough. We begin to grow restless after the Queen's speech or when we wake from the afternoon nap to confront Billy Smart's circus. There's the clearing up to be done, the hunt for the lost present in the dustbin among the wrappings. The Christmas tree suddenly looks redundant. It's there for another twelve days and already beginning to shed its pine needles. There is something you're supposed to spray on it along with the frosting. It comes out of an aerosol can like cream these days. There ought to be something one can spray on oneself, 'spirit of Christmas, do not store near heat'.

Boxing Day and yesterday's papers, yesterday's luncheon too. Everything closed up waiting for the all clear and when will that be exactly? you ask yourself. There are things happening, of course, unthinkable things like football matches and morning greyhound races and sponsored walks. People will do anything when they are bored, even gardening, but for us creative chaps, nothing. 'For heaven's sake sit down and pay the bills or write your thank you letters,' they urge. But unless everyone else is working flat out I am quite unable to put key to paper. Most mornings, I tell myself, it is better to sit in front of a typewriter and shuffle the keys than to have had to have got up three hours earlier to cut up meat. But today butchers have hung up their boaters and their aprons are in the spin dryers. Will they be back tomorrow or will I? Last week there was no time, this week there is nothing but time. This year they asked me to play Hook in *Peter Pan*. We'll help you down the ladders, they told me, and along the plank, of course, and if you are going to double Mr Darling, we'll have slightly older children and a larger kennel. I told them no at the time, but now I am not so sure. Besides the salary at the end of the week there would have been something to do like learning to walk with a wooden leg, which might come in useful too the way the traffic is.

Of course, there are always the presents to play with. I've made my list and now we shall have to see. There is a clock which lights up when you clap your hands, it's called the slave clock and I saw it in New York but was too mean to buy it. I don't suppose it's reached these shores yet. I put in for some new executive toy not a puzzle, I cannot do puzzles and give in at once like crosswords. I haven't the gift. Just to remind myself of the fact, I sometimes look at clue one down in the morning paper – if I get this, I tell myself, I might have a go. But it's always the same, I simply can't get started. Last year I got a box of wooden sardines you were supposed to empty them out and put them back in the tin. They are still free in a neat pile on the dressing-table. People will give me books on gambling and horse racing. I don't want to read them; when I can afford it I like to go in person to Sandown or a casino. About the day after the day after Boxing Day my wife will ask me if I am going to put away the bath oil and the ties. I love bath oil but the ties I get seem to sting like those mysterious invisible fleas in the water off Bora Bora. The ties tend to depress me, I find myself worrying about the life style of the donors, they can't be happy I tell myself, they couldn't have been concentrating when they chose this one, there must be some awful gnawing secret sorrow of which I know nothing. The grandchildren's presents are best, the tooth picks, the cloth to clean the lens of my spectacles, the chocolate orange. Then, of course, there's Daisy, my newest granddaughter. This will be her first Christmas and I am hoping for something really sensational from her. My present is a cot fitment from Sweden. If you fix it right, it converts her sleeping quarters into a sort of private gymnasium – I just hope she doesn't reciprocate with one of those appalling stationary bicycles.

The Contemporary Arthurian

As a card-carrying member of American Express, I was delighted and indeed entitled to receive a letter only last week from Mr J. S. Quarterly, our resident Vice-President in Brighton. Obviously Mr Quarterly is still some way from assuming supreme command of the American Express empire but a resident Vice-President would, I think, be roughly the equivalent of a Vice-Consul when we British were top dogs. Not yet a fully fledged Consul, let alone President, but all systems go and climbing.

The first sentence of the letter immediately arrested my attention. 'Here is some news I believe will be of great interest to you.' So this then was not to be a casual communication bringing me the gossip of piers and pavilion, and possibly the new marina, but something more personal – and so it was to prove. 'The International Arthurian Society,' and I think Mr Quarterly did well to stress the international, 'has decided to commemorate its thirtieth anniversary by commissioning for its members an exclusive collection of six English bone china plates each depicting,' and I quote, 'one of the most famous scenes from what is surely the greatest legend of all time, King Arthur and the Knights of the Round Table.' Mr Quarterly thinks it is important for me to note that each plate's subject was chosen by three of the most eminent experts on Arthurian history: Professor Menard of the Sorbonne, Professor Molk of Gottingen and our own Professor Pickford of Hull. Never having previously collected bone china and having only the haziest recollection of the Arthurian legend, I seem to remember a sword sticking out of a lake and a musical comedy which featured an enormous English sheep dog. I am naturally delighted to find myself afforded privileges normally reserved for Old Arthurians, delighted but not surprised. After all we card-carrying members know we have only to wave the card in the faces of *maître d'hôtels* and airline receptionists to be afforded the attention and service once granted to Viceroys. Nor is cash demanded on this occasion, only a brief questionnaire to be completed along with the order form thoughtfully enclosed, together with full colour reproductions of the plates themselves. There is a stern warning that the former is valid only if postmarked by 15 October and I must understand that not more than two sets can be ordered. Furthermore, no plates will be sold in stores or art galleries and in future the only way a person wishing to acquire the collection can hope to do so will be by finding an original owner who can be persuaded to sell. I find this a shade sinister. What if some crazed plate-hungry collector should discover my name in the records and unleash the heavy mob to call personally. 'We have ways of taking your plate.' Then again breakages do occur. There used to be six, I hear myself remarking, but, alas, the one depicting Vivianne the Beautiful Enchantress weaving a spell around the Wizard Merlin entrapping him for ever in a prison whose walls are invisible, disintegrated when hung by the washing machine.

I should be sorry to lose Vivianne who wears a clinging see-through bikini and seems to have captured old Merlin with a surfeit of apples which lie around him at the base of the tree, under which he is resting clutching his wand in one hand and, unless I am mistaken, about to clutch his temptress with the other. I really must read the book, or better still watch the new BBC series about to be delivered, like the plates, in six instalments.

Of course, I could get all the plates, apparently, in one fell swoop in time for Christmas, in which case I must be prepared to be charged the £198 in full upon despatch; or I could receive one every six weeks on the understanding I could return one, or all, of them after fifteen days and I can cancel my subscription at any time on the further understanding that once cancelled, it can never be reinstated. Quite apart from postal breakages, the whole operation seems fraught with peril on both sides. What if I and all the subscribers tend to reject Lancelot secretly in love with Queen Guinevere and wearing her colours on his helmet defeating Melegant who has treacherously abducted the Queen. I don't say we will, mind you, but we just might. What would Eugene Vinavier, our Honorary President, and the L'Atelies Art Editions Ltd. do with them them? Have we guarantees they will never be resold as matching ash trays?

Which brings up the dilemma we shall all face sooner or later – are we to use the chinaware as side or cake plates or to buy a period Welsh Dresser on which to display them? I could be content, I think, with one. Tristan and Isolde in the forest after the escape from the Castle of King Mark, Isolde's husband. Isolde is wearing roughly the same costume as Vivianne, although on her it is marginally less revealing. On the other hand, she is a good deal younger and there is a rather beautiful peeping stag about to witness the lovemaking. But there is no hint of which plate will be the first in the post and I might have to pay for all the others before I collected my prize. I suppose, as is my custom on these occasions, I shall dither and procrastinate until the fateful day arrives when my mind is made up for me on 16 October bereft for ever of the opportunity to pass the chocolate cake resting temporarily on the visage of King Arthur, the once and future King being borne off mortally wounded to the mysterious Isle of Avalon by his fair ladies in mourning. On the other hand, supposing the cake remains uneaten, none of us will know what we've missed.

Even if, as seems probable, I have not on this occasion participated to any financial extent in the venture, I have an absurd desire to be present at the ceremony which will take place when the exact number of subscribed collections have been completed and all masters will be destroyed in the presence of Mr Eric Demierre, public notary in Geneva. I might even be allowed to strike the first blow.

Country Life

I had seen the cottage advertised in *The Times* but it proved not all that easy to find without signposts. When I did so, I bought it at once from the owner who was on his knees finishing the floor tiling. I knocked £50 off his price and he got up with a smile and shook my hand.

A man called Slyfield owned the nine acres I wished to add to my two – he came to tea and opined it was too wet to tramp the boundaries.

'It's no good to me,' he said, 'I've taken the timber.'

'I need it,' I told him, 'for the right of way and because someone else might build on it one day.'

'No one will build, lad,' he assured me, 'it's not building land and never could be. Give me what you think is right.'

'It's worth a lot to me,' I said, 'I'd rather you told me what it's worth to you now you've taken out the timber,' I nudged gently.

'Two hundred and fifty.'

'An acre?' I asked.

'No, no, that's for the lot.' I never saw him again and although I paid him and the builder I am for ever in their debt.

In Berkshire's debt too, I suppose. My parents had a house in the grounds of Wellington College during the first great war and when it was over they sent me to school there. Blackwater, Sandhurst and Bracknell are still as deadly for me as the Bermuda Triangle. I am not even completely at my ease in Reading but all the rest of Berkshire is safe. Beautiful and safe. Why else should the Sultan of Oman choose to be my neighbour? And Dave Allen live across the fields? I see him once a year, perhaps, but the Sultan never. I know a man who knows him and this year he lent me a pony trap to head the parade during Festival Week. His mother, the Sultana, rides slowly behind her daughters past the house; she in a massive and, for all I know, bullet-proof Daimler, the girls on horseback attended by individual grooms. There is no thought of a pace faster than a slow march. I dream sometimes of the Sultan coming to tea bearing gifts but so far he keeps his distance. His palace is floodlit and guarded and when he comes, they say, it is sometimes with the King of Jordan himself. On either side of the road we share are two giant oak trees. 'You'll never live to see them shake hands,' I was told when I came here first. But now their branches are entwined as they await the camel train which, when petrol finally gives out, must one day pass beneath.

Not all Berkshire is quite as exotic as Crazies' Hill, which is the name they gave us when some eccentric bought the town hall at Henley and moved it stone by stone to where it now stands. He never lived in it. Rumour has it he just wanted it out of the way, but in that case, why bother to re-erect it? Less puzzling is Rebecca's Well, the waters of which are supposed to cure diseases of the liver. Because of frogs which live to an incredible old age in the basin, my children, and now my grandchildren, fill their medicine bottles there, carry them home, write down a wish and drop it within. Only if the water turns pink overnight will their wish be granted, but up to now we have had 100 per cent success.

As I've said, I came here first when the signposts had been removed and if you asked your way to the Post Office careful villagers would stoutly refuse the information. We took the war seriously but one evening when things were at their blackest with bombs falling, although I hasten to say not on us, and invasion was apparently expected hourly, we took ourselves, my wife and I, for a swim in the river, encroaching as was our custom on the waters of the Wargrave Yacht Club. On the lawn a solitary sailor, dressed impecccably in ducks and blazer, finished his afternoon tea and, loosening the painter of his dinghy, proceeded to scull himself upstream. He was almost out of sight when a man came running breathless along the bank from the clubhouse and hailed the departing Sinbad. 'Commodore', he yelled through the megaphone, 'Are you going ashore? If so I'll haul down your flag.'

In a moment, down came the ensign and then, surprisingly, an even more splendid standard fluttered at the mast-head

We kept the flag flying in those days and we still do. For the second year running Wargrave is judged the tidiest village in Berkshire. There are other villages round about with arguably prettier names and certainly prettier houses than mine, but there can be few towns more beautiful than Henley. It was here for some years that my mother-in-law, Gladys, had a house on the regatta course. I remember one Friday afternoon, before the fun had really begun and while the preliminary heats were being decided, getting up from a deck-chair on her lawn to observe the progress of a Russian oarsman struggling lengths behind his rival.

His progress was observed by a fellow fixing tiles on our roof. This was the first year the Russians had been back since the war and my companion was in no doubt of the fate awaiting the oarsman in imminent defeat. 'Buck up, Popoff,' he chided, 'for Heaven's sake buck up! They'll shoot you when you get home!'

A flock of Canada Geese now grazes the water meadows and a flight of pilots has alighted on the new building estate, but I remember when Britain's premier test pilot decided to make his home here. I greeted him with some advice on where to shop and introduced him to the local barber, a close friend whose establishment was not easy to find, being located in his kitchen. A bachelor, he liked to keep an eye on his lunch cooking on the stove. Wondering if my advice had been followed and possibly hoping for an extra slice of corned beef, I enquired of the local grocer whether the gallant captain had opened his account. 'Indeed yes,' I was told, 'for as long as it lasts.'

It was about this time that I got myself reported for careless talk and my oldest friend in the village, the special constable-cum-electrician, arrived to inform me that two officers from the Special Branch had that morning called on him to check my potential danger to the realm. 'In Bournemouth recently you told a friend as yet unidentified, "I don't mind having my back against a wall, just find me a wall".' I was speaking in sorrow, I assured him, not of the war but of the box office.

'I told them,' said my friend, 'that you were a nutter' – it was the first time I had ever heard the word – 'but if it happens again, you know, they could call you up.' Years later my friend, who had the least suspicious mind of anyone I had known, let alone a policeman, picked up two burglars unaided after a particularly successful local foray and drove them to the station. The railway station.

Berkshire has other ancient monuments besides myself: it has castles and ruins, atomic power stations and the two best racecourses in the world. It has exquisitely named villages and public houses. It is remote and at the same time accessible and its roots go very deep. The people don't change Berkshire but Berkshire quite often changes them. Lord

Barrymore built a theatre here and the Rhodes family once owned the land for miles around and created an entirely self-supporting community.

When I came here first I used to try sometimes to hang a picture and marvel at the havoc created by falling plaster, but I have grown cautious over the years and have also, of course, strengthened my foundations from time to time. That's the lesson Berkshire teaches us all.

The Happy Punter

Whoever granted the licences for casinos in Britain was in the first instance at least an ex-colonial administrator used to putting down the natives. On what must have been an exceedingly brief leave, he took a short walk through London's West End and designated the sites. 'Carlton House Terrace, of course,' he told his officials on his brisk reconnaissance, 'and then I think on to Berkeley Square.' What about Soho? someone must have asked him. 'A couple if you must and if people still go there now the Empire is a cinema, but the Square is more suitable. We'll have three in the Square. 'And the rest? they asked. 'Scatter them around as far as Park Lane, Curzon Street, Hill Street, Park Street. The idea is a chap should be able to walk from one to another? Like Vegas? they asked him. 'Not exactly,' he told them, 'no song and dance, food perhaps and drink, as long as they don't spill the stuff on the green baize.'

By the time he had moved further West there wasn't much left to hand out. One near Harrods, two if you must, and one in the Cromwell Road, they won't be able to stop but we must do something for the underprivileged. How about Harrogate? We should have one there. Preston? someone asked. 'I've never heard of it,' he told them. 'I hope I never shall.'

Mind you, I have no quarrel with the ex-brigadier and I never have been able to stop at the one in the Cromwell Road, hopefully called the Mint. But oh, the happy hours I have had at nearly all the others. Now I come to think of it, someone must have told him that there was another side to the park and persuaded him to scatter a few in that direction, one even in the Tottenham Court Road itself and a couple more further West but these for me have always lacked the elegance of Crockfords or the Ritz and one at least resembles a converted pool hall.

Gambling for me has always been a mousetrap, not one of those where a nibble on the cheese can break my back but the kind where the trapdoor closes and I have to beg to be let out. Every now and then I take a cautious bite on the gorgonzola and evade the mechanism. I actually leave with a bit more of the cheese than I took in. After a time I grow over-confident, spring the trap and panic. Released, I write to the secretaries and demand I shall never again be permitted on their premises but of course I don't post the letters for fear they might take me seriously.

There is in Britain a society unlisted in the telephone book called the Beaumont Society which looks after transvestites. I once asked the secretary what advice he gave to new members. 'I tell them,' he replied, 'that however ashamed they may feel the morning after, *never* throw it away. Otherwise they are sure to be shopping again before long. It's compulsive, you see, like gambling.' How true. As is so often the case I have my own theory of what makes a gambler. It is the desire nearly everyone experiences for change. Quite simply I want to be someone else. I am not prepared, as some are, to change my profession or even my sex but I want to experience danger and remorse and to be at times even a bigger idiot than I am in real life. On matinée days I love to go round the front after a performance, withdraw my share of the take from the box office and hurry to one or other of the establishments nearby. If, as is often the case, I lose more than I have earned by pulling faces and making a fool of myself from 2.30 till 5.00, not including of course the income tax I already owe, I am strangely content and work harder that evening in the theatre.

I have done what most gamblers like to do: go away and come back. Of course normally I don't do all that well at matinées so the sum involved is never catastrophic. The atmosphere in Soho is different from, say, the Ritz. Here most of us are in the catering trades, a few actors, a lot of waiters and, of course, the Chinese. The Chinese are the most elegant players and, if you doubt my word, go to Macao and watch them playing *fan tan* in their own territory. *Fan tan* is *chemin de fer* played with pearl buttons. Not that they've heard of it at Crockfords, the beautiful house in Carlton House Terrace which has been a gambling club for more than two centuries. It used to be bridge and backgammon and it still is but now it's all the fun of the fair, though they seem to have got rid of the craps table. Most of the others have followed suit: for one thing it requires a large staff to man one; and for another, they say the Arabs found it rather too noisy. Most of the clubs in the West End are Arab orientated. I remember one evening going into what was at that time my local and finding kings and princes from Kuwait or Saudia betting £7,000 on a number of the roulette wheel and not just on the number but all round it. When they guessed right they won a quarter of a million pounds and if, as sometimes happens, the number repeated they were half a million up. But the club stood its ground and gradually they melted away. You can't really win at roulette unless you limit your time and take a profit however small – but where is the fun in that? Once in Vegas I played solidly for six hours and across the table a little old lady argued every spin and outstayed me. Next morning I asked the croupiers why they had been so patient with the old relic. 'She owns the joint,' the told me. 'Her husband died and left her the business.'

Every card-carrying gambler needs three or four different clubs to suit his mood. Who am I today? I ask myself. Onassis? I am off to the Ritz. A little old lady from Chelsea? And I find myself in Knightsbridge. A head water? A bookmaker? A sheik? It's all imagination, I suppose. Onassis owned the casino in Monte Carlo. Sitting in the Hotel de Paris and espying an acquaintance he asked him why he hadn't been in the rooms all summer long. The friend explained. It seems he had strolled over from a hugely successful evening at the baccarat table and plonked an enormous bet on the roulette wheel. In his excitement the croupier spun the ball too hard and it spun off on to the carpet. In disgust Mr Onassis's acquaintance removed his chips. The croupier then spun his number and the officials pointed out they couldn't pay on a previous throw. My argument, the gambler explained, was that wasn't the previous throw, that was the throw. He hadn't, of course, a leg to stand on but Mr Onassis enquired how much he would have won, took the half million or so out of his pocket and paid him.

'See you this evening', he told the happy punter and, no doubt, he did.

Life at the Big Top

Some time ago I became a member of the Punch Table. Mr Punch, as English as roast beef, always lunches on a Wednesday and, if you are lucky enough to write for the paper for some years, you may one day be afforded what to me is the inestimable privilege of carving your initials alongside those of Mark Twain and Jerome K. Jerome and invite yourself to lunch every Wednesday for the rest of your life.

It is a heady privilege and a great honour and perhaps I shouldn't be boasting about it all but for the fact that the editor told me to write about circuses. We had been discussing circuses of which, like most other matters, I have had a passing but by no means profound knowledge ever since my childhood when I fondly imagined that all the passengers on the bus for Piccadilly Circus would soon be enjoying the performance without me.

Nothing works out as you think it's going to, and this is one of those mornings when having sat down to write about Barnum and possibly Bailey, Mr Chipperfield, Mr Smart and Lord John Sanger, I feel an urge to write about something slightly different – what in the ringing tones of countless presidents has been announced as the state of the nation. My nation or as much mine as anyone else's after seventy years and a whale of a time.

Since I was a young man – and we may as well start with the audience suitably arranged on tiers some with soft seats, some with hard – the appearance and indeed the standard of life in circuses has changed very much for the better. In a way I have been part of the circus and in the years between the wars travelled as circus performers must from town to town all over this country. Those were the days when a good many children went barefoot and some had rickets.

Those were the days when to go abroad for a holiday was the privilege of the very few, the most the rest could hope for was a few days in lodgings at the seaside. Those were the days when to be out of work (and hundreds of thousands were) was not only to go hungry yourself but see your children go hungry. Hence the rickets. Well, that's not the case today. The standard of life has risen considerably and I believe continues to rise. Economic experts may not agree with me but they must surely concede that it is on the whole a far happier and fairer society than it used to be. We may have been richer in our history but we have seldom been wiser in our provision of the health service, pensions, education, unemployment benefits. If you tell me that by providing all this at the expense of the state we discourage people from foraging on their own and that we encourage the layabouts of our society. I would answer that, as in British justice, it is better that a hundred guilty should go free than that one innocent man should hang. Besides which, every society needs its layabouts just like every school is sustained not by its conformist prize winners but by its rebels. In the perpetual sheep dog trials staged by the educational authorities it is not the shepherd whistling to his dog to herd the obedient into the pen, it is the black sheep who breaks away and may or may not eventually be induced to join the flock that makes the spectacle so amusing.

But never mind the audience, let's get back to the ring where it's all supposed to be happening. This is not as big a circus as it used to be, there are no longer three rings, only one, we no longer have the troupe of Indian tigers, the performing African lions, the American buffaloes or their eagles. The ringmaster is better dressed than most of the performers but it is well to remember he wears borrowed clothes and he is careful never to crack his whip. Just announce the acts and hope to God they will perform.

In Britain recently you may have caught the performance on one of its bad days. Immediately after Christmas we had the sales and that seemed a good time for the band to strike up and the clowns to appear but almost at once things seemed to go wrong. Mr Callaghan's Trade Union equestrian act misfired. The old carthorse refused to canter and even so experienced a bareback rider as Mr Len Murray lost his footing, on what many people feel is now an ancient and rather ungainly steed. In the ensuing confusion the show very nearly refused to go on at all. In the time available it was barely possible to rig the safety net under the family N.U.P.E. and to persuade this assorted troupe of gravediggers, hospital ancillary workers, dustmen and water maintenance engineers into continuing the performance. Even so many argued that with a net so high the whole tent might cave in on performers and spectators alike and eager volunteers jumped into the ring to add to the *mêlée* and try if possible to wrest the clothes off the ringmaster's back. On one point everyone seemed to agree: this is no way to run a circus and already a queue of wealthy foreigners was beginning to form at the box-office windows demanding their money back, or cancelling their advance bookings.

But most of us will have to stay under the big top and just sweat it out as we have so often done in the past. The British people simply do not believe that the poles will snap or the canvas be blown inside out and we have good reason for our faith. We have the lesson of history behind us – more than a thousand years during which, despite temptation to do so, we have not torn ourselves apart but grown slowly, painfully, hesitatingly closer together. The temptation to do just that is still there, often fanned by the media, continuously stoked by the politicians and the zealots on the far right and the far left.

We have never lost our belief in our own destiny. Not many years ago nor for the first time, did this country save herself by her exertions and Europe by her example.

But on this occasion, you may argue, if we British are as anxious as all that to set Europe an example, why don't we, having joined them in the Common Market, take a leaf out of their book and adopt some of their admittedly more up-to-date methods of production and ways of improving industrial relations. The short answer is that while every foreigner looks alike to us and, for all we know, is, no two Englishmen ever look alike to each other. We have all the disadvantages of the class system for which, though we have in some measure benefited in the past, we are now furiously engaged in disposing of as quickly as possible. Some think that with successive Labour governments this process might have accelerated and it is the disappointment and frustration of the under-privileged and underpaid that lie at the root of our present difficulty. The nation is deeply divided between those that argue that until we produce more wealth we cannot afford to improve the conditions of those who must rely on the welfare state and those who argue that, given a more satisfactory welfare state, envy, hatred and malice will cease to gum up the works.

In my view the donkey works better when he has eaten the carrot provided he is still fairly hungry and our lower paid workers are likely to stay fairly hungry for many years to come. What we need is for the driver of the cart to get out and walk alongside us and on occasions push.

Henry Irving, the greatest of all circus clowns was asked towards the end of a long life what he had got for himself out of all the effort he had put into life. A few friends, the great actor replied, and a whisky and soda whenever I wanted one. What else is there to get? Yet the pursuit of money is still the British national pastime. No one ever seems to tire of it. Yet what matters at the end of the day to rich and poor alike is not wealth but happiness. And happiness is something very different, it is not the things money can buy but nearly always the things it can't.

The man who wrote that a little rebellion now and then is a good thing also wrote that the tree of Liberty must be refreshed from time to time with the blood of patriots and tyrants – it is its natural manure. And he went on to write that we hold these truths self-evident, that all men are created equal, that they are endowed by their Creator with inalienable rights; that among these are life, liberty and the pursuit of happiness.

Thomas Jefferson knew what it was all about.

Dukeophilia

Whenever Father met a duke, he would always try to borrow money from him and, as he could seldom afford to pay him back, clubland for me in earlier times was waiting with him at the top of the stairs of the Orleans or Boodles to see if it was wise to descend.

When the money supply ran out, we were off to Attenborough's, the pawnbrokers in Oxford Street but, though he took pains to introduce me to the nobility, he used to make me wait under the golden balls while he pledged the canteen. One of his creditors in those days was the Duke of Westminster and Father was always bringing him into the conversation. No one ever called Westminster anything but Bendor just as today the Duke of Devonshire is called Andy. I sat beside him the other day at that long luncheon table at the Dorchester where dukes go in winter time when they are not in Barbados to present trophies or receive cheques. I was careful to call him 'Your Grace'. Not too often, of course. As with royalty, it doesn't do to overdo it. 'Your Majesty' the first time and then simply 'Ma'am'.

The trouble with the class system where we Dukeophiles are concerned is that we simply can't get enough of it. We are not properly organized; nor are they. If you want to look at an old steam engine or some other fellow's collection of bottle tops you can join a society and go it together. But Society itself is different. I doubt if there is a single collector who has all the signatures of the peerage except possibly the fellow who gets them to sign on at Westminster when they show up for their attendance money. Of course if some enterprising business man got them together and had them autograph a tea tray, it would sell like hot cakes. Hot cakes! That's what they are in my book and if you were to ask why what on earth is different about a duke – or an earl for that matter – I would answer, nothing, and that is the whole point. Dukes are exactly the same as you or me in the human stamp catalogue unless you happen, like me, to be a collector. Then they are different.

Just as a man may stand in a reed bed for hours in the hope of sighting a Siberian Mallard, so I will wait dry martini in hand scanning the other VIPs within the enclosure at a Foyle's Literary Luncheon hoping to catch a glimpse of, say, the Duke of Bedford. The Duke of Bedford wasn't exactly born a duke. None of them are unless they arrive posthumously if that is not a contradiction in terms. Dukes start life as someone else entirely and only when the parent bird dies do they become fully fledged and sprout the ermine and the coronet. I dined the other night with a man my host referred to as David Somerset and who I think one day may become the Duke of Beaufort, though I haven't verified the matter as I don't want to be disappointed. He could be merely a younger son or – although he looked a great deal healthier and far younger than I – die before he succeeds. As a collector I took great pleasure in his company. I have a natural affinity with the aristocracy although I do not meet them nearly as often as I would wish. On the other hand life peers mean absolutely nothing in my life. As the Baroness Dacre was reported to have announced when Hugh Trevor Roper temporarily usurped her family name and decided in future that he wanted to be a Dacre himself, 'It's simply not worth worrying what life peers get up to.'

Sometimes I ask myself whether I would have made a good duke. The question, of course, is academic but I have a suspicion that had I been born on a mulberry leaf I might have gone at it a little too hard. Dukes seldom adopt any other profession. For them enough is enough: they don't go on the stage or in to the law and as far as I know there isn't a single noble chartered accountant. True, they join boards of directors and become patrons of Otter Conservation Trusts but when they do consent to dabble in – and on occasions it must be admitted cloud – the waters, it is seldom for ready cash. They remain aloof.

It may seem unfair that they should have inherited the earth in and around Pimlico, castles and safari parks, grouse moors and the Elgin Marbles but look what happens when they dispose of their treasures. How many of us today would willingly accept an invitation to stay at Mentmore Towers? The last thing any of us would want when we visit Woburn is to have to cart any of the contents home except on a picture postcard. Like the pools, dukes play their harmless necessary part in our society. Whenever I meet one of those rare creatures, I feel a curious tingling sensation at the nape of the neck. I experience exitement. I do not seek to question why but, like most Englishmen in our class-ridden society, I am grateful. Every so often some foreign busybodies profess themselves aghast at our class-ridden society claiming we would do better in the market-place without it. Quite apart from the fact that there then would be no one suitable at the next coronation to carry the Royal Galosh, we couldn't have a coronation at all.

A constitutional monarchy can only survive as long as there are humble, grateful and obedient snobs to support it. I am proud to be one of them.